MW00449368

The CBT Couples Toolbox

Over 45 Exercises to Improve Communication, Navigate Problems, and Build Strong Relationships

John W. Ludgate, Ph.D. Tereza N. Grubr, M.A.

Copyright © 2018 by John W. Ludgate and Tereza N. Grubr

Published by
PESI Publishing & Media
PESI, Inc
3839 White Ave
Eau Claire, WI 54703

Cover: Amy Rubenzer
Layout: Bookmasters & Amy Rubenzer

ISBN: 9781683731023

All rights reserved.

Printed in the United States of America.

PESI
Publishing
& Media
www.publishing.pesi.com

About the Authors

John W. Ludgate, PhD, is a licensed psychologist, who has worked as a psychotherapist for almost 30 years. He currently works at the CBT Center of Western North Carolina, located in Asheville, NC. He specializes in treating mood, anxiety, relationship and psychosexual disorders. As well as having an active clinical practice, he is involved in training and supervision in CBT.

He obtained a Bachelor's degree in Psychology from Trinity College, Dublin, a Master's degree in Clinical Psychology from University of Edinburgh in Scotland and a Ph.D. from Trinity College, Dublin. He trained at the Center for Cognitive Therapy under Dr. Aaron Beck, the founder of Cognitive Therapy, obtaining a Post-Doctoral Fellowship in Cognitive Therapy from the University of Pennsylvania in 1986. He subsequently became assistant director of training at Dr. Beck's Center. In the early 1990's Dr. Ludgate was a Research Clinical Psychologist at the University of Oxford in England and served as a cognitive-behavioral therapist in several outcome studies of panic disorder, agoraphobia, social phobia and hypochondriasis. He subsequently worked as a clinical psychologist in state agencies and private practice.

In 1988 he published the book *Maximizing Psychotherapeutic Gains and Preventing Relapse in Emotionally Distressed Clients* and was co-editor with Beck and others of *Cognitive Therapy with Inpatients: Developing a Cognitive Milieu* published in 1990. He published *Cognitive-Behavioral Therapy and Relapse Prevention for Depression and Anxiety* in 2009 and *Heal Yourself: A CBT Approach to Reducing Therapist Distress and Increasing Therapeutic Effectiveness* in 2012. In 2014 he co-authored the book *Overcoming Compassion Fatigue: A Practical Resilience Workbook* with Martha Teater. In 2016 he co-edited the book *Teaching and Supervising Cognitive Behavioral Therapy* published by Wiley. He has written numerous journal articles and book chapters in the field of Cognitive Behavior Therapy for Anxiety and Depression. He has presented many seminars and workshops on cognitive behavioral approaches, both nationally and internationally.

He is a Founding Fellow of the Academy of Cognitive Therapy and serves on the Credentialing Committee of the Academy.

Tereza N. Grubr, MA, LPCA has worked in the field of mental health counseling, both inpatient and outpatient, for almost 10 years. In addition to receiving training in psychotherapy during her Master Degree in Psychology, Tereza has received extensive training in CBT through the CBT Center of WNC. She has, also, been extensively trained in positive psychology which she is passionate about and frequently incorporates into her work. Tereza currently works as an outpatient mental health therapist at Family Preservation Services of North Carolina.

Contents

Introduction

This is an exciting time to be working in the psychotherapy field. Over the years we have witnessed a fascinating evolution of **interrelated treatment approaches for overcoming suffering**. None of these approaches—whether Cognitive Behavioral Therapy, Motivational Interviewing, Positive Psychology, or Mindfulness-Based approaches—works in a vacuum. **Enduring change requires the engagement of the whole being through behavior, cognition, honest inquiry and reflection, awareness of one's strengths, and a non-judging attitude.** In truth, it is the **integrative way in which these concepts work together that creates a synergy bigger than the sum** of its parts. It's no surprise that clinicians who work with relationship issues are looking for hands-on, practical tools or protocols that embrace this broader, integrative perspective. That's exactly why we wrote this book!

The CBT Couples Toolbox **combines complementary treatment approaches, such as Cognitive Behavioral Therapy (CBT), Behavior Therapy, Dialectical Behavior Therapy (DBT) and Acceptance and Commitment Therapy (ACT), in a practical, therapist-friendly way.**

No longer will you need to access multiple resources for using CBT and other 'CBT friendly' approaches. Our hope is that this workbook will help fill the gap between traditional couples' therapy and other techniques in psychotherapy such as Motivational Interviewing, Mindfulness and Positive Psychology. What is more, the step-by-step strategies and techniques in this workbook are not only intended for couples' therapy; they can also be easily adapted for use in individual therapy.

YOUR INTEGRATIVE ROADMAP

Any journey makes sense if you understand the roadmap. For *The CBT Couples Toolbox*, we've crafted a roadmap that will help you to successfully navigate working with these approaches in an effective and seamless way. As you will see, this journey takes you from your initial session and facilitating change to using the different treatment approaches. Along the way, it will become clear as to how to integrate these ideas.

Chapter 1, **Assessment and Conceptualization,** explores the assessment of clients' problems from the initial session in a very detailed manner. You'll find useful outlining measures and interview questions to pinpoint issues. A conceptualization system using the cognitive-behavioral model is offered and CBT treatment planning is outlined to get things clearly on track.

Chapter 2, **Client Engagement,** examines the issues of evaluating clients' motivation for change in themselves and their relationship. Here you'll examine important change tools, from the stages of change model to motivational interviewing strategies, and others. These early-in-therapy tools of engagement are designed to optimize client change and pave the way for the work ahead.

Chapter 3, **Cognitive Behavioral Therapy (CBT) Strategies,** utilizes CBT strategies to encourage change in cognition and beliefs. This includes increasing awareness of perceptions of each other, embedded beliefs about the relationship, and assumptions about change or thoughts about themselves.

Chapter 4, **Behavioral Interventions,** provides evidence-based behavioral methods for making substantive changes in communication, assertiveness, and conflict resolution.

Chapter 5, **DBT, Mindfulness and Related Interventions,** describes DBT approaches such as validation and emotional regulation—skills that are useful for couples' high levels of conflict. You'll also find acceptance and mindfulness strategies, as well as compassion-focused procedures that foster a more understanding attitude and caring behavior towards partners.

Chapter 6, **Positive Psychology Interventions,** consists of exercises and practices from expressing gratitude and practicing benevolence to developing positive rituals and engaging in self-care—all of which have been shown to increase positive and pro-relationship behaviors. They are also helpful in re-framing conflict and problems by offering a more strength-based perspective.

As you prepare to embark on this journey, it might be helpful to start with the core concepts for getting started in Chapters 1 and 2. Afterwards, feel free to move around the roadmap and explore various chapters. You may already be familiar with certain areas and want to incorporate new strategies by exploring those first, in more depth.

We encourage you to reproduce and use the worksheets in this book to facilitate therapy with couples. We have developed these tools over many years of clinical practice and our clients have found them most helpful in the journey toward change. They often support and elaborate on the work done in sessions and optimize learning which in turn creates the conditions for change.

Our experience in conducting training in CBT is therapists value these worksheets, handouts and forms, often as much as or even more than other aspects of training, so we decided to enrich this workbook with customized forms and worksheets that can guide practice in applying skills both inside and between therapy session. We hope you find them practical and helpful in your everyday practice in treating couples

CHAPTER 1:
Assessment and Conceptualization

While your personal style or approach can determine to some extent the content and process of the initial interview, in Cognitive Behavioral Therapy and allied approaches, there is a structure and agenda which is important in the initial sessions. These matter because they are designed to help you identify problems and assist in the treatment planning process.

METHODS OF ASSESSMENT

By utilizing rating scales, interviews, questionnaires and direct observation, you will gain a tremendous amount of valuable information. In our own work with couples, for example, we routinely begin with standard scales and inventories. Why would we do that? Here are four good reasons for using them:

1. They serve as an initial exercise for couples, and you will have a direct demonstration of how couples work together on a shared task.

2. They give you insight into how couples respond emotionally to each other's ratings. You will observe each person's emotional range. Are they capable of empathy and other emotions? In addition, you can see how emotion is expressed or triggered.

3. They provide a measure of relationship dysfunction and can help you more clearly pinpoint areas that need work. This can provide a basis for mutual exploration and development of a treatment plan.

4. They can be repeated and serve as an outcome measure or index of progress. Giving clients evidence of how far they have come can be both motivating and reinforcing.

The following scales have been used extensively and found to be useful in working with couples. Although the word "marital" is used in two of these scales, couples don't need to be married to benefit from these:

- **Dyadic Adjustment Scale (DAS).** This measure includes areas of disagreement, frequency of specific problems, beliefs about the future of the relationship, feelings about the partner/relationship and frequency of positives. It involves four factors: dyadic satisfaction, dyadic cohesion, dyadic consensus and affectional expression. (Spanier, 1976)

- **Marital Satisfaction Inventory (MSI).** This measures overall satisfaction plus areas of specific dissatisfaction. It was revised in 1999 following the initial version in 1981. (Snyder & Aikman, 1999)

- **Marital Happiness Scale (MHS).** This scale has 10 items which measure current levels of happiness with different areas of the relationship including money, household responsibilities, communication, rearing of children, sex and other dimensions of a relationship. (Azrin, Naster & Jones, 1973)

Some of these instruments and other useful relationship and couple assessment measures can be found in Fisher & Corcoran's (1994) *Measures for Clinical Practice* and these instruments are reviewed in Dattilio's (2010) *Cognitive-Behavioral Therapy with Couples and Families*.

Conduct the First Interview

One of the key questions that couple's therapists must face is how to conduct the initial interview. Should this be done separately or with the couple together? There are pros and cons of each strategy.

Conducting part of the initial interview separately has the following advantages:

- It can be more comfortable and feel safer for the clients when conflict is high.
- There may be more honesty due to less fear of repercussions. Stating concerns to the therapist in front of a partner can be daunting if there has been abuse.
- It is easier for you, as a clinician, to manage and obtain information.
- You can assess in more depth each individual's perception of the problem, as well as their views about themselves, their partner and the relationship.
- It allows for an exploration of any personal items clients may feel reluctant to share in joint session, such as a history of abuse or details of past relationships.
- It can allow for an assessment of personal psychopathology such as depression, substance abuse and personality disorder, which have ramifications on the relationship.

Conducting individual assessments can also have the following disadvantages:

- It is time consuming and may delay the intervention phase.
- It may encourage "secret sharing" and leave one or more partners feeling that the therapist has taken sides.
- If the couple are not seen together, an opportunity to observe the couple's interactive style, as information is gathered, is missed.

That brings us to the second scenario of conducting a joint assessment. Here are some key advantages for using this strategy:

- The couple's communication patterns are clearly observed as they discuss their problems.
- Signs of affection, support and understanding in those initial sessions can be noted.
- You get an initial impression of characteristic interaction patterns in the couple (for example, one talks more or one is more critical).
- This offers an opportunity to note how each individual's memories or perceptions of the same events differ and, most importantly, how they respond to any discrepancies.
- Both clients can feel heard and build shared rapport with the therapist.

Because of the advantages of both approaches, **we favor a blended version which involves the couple being seen together in the first assessment session, and then separately for two subsequent individual assessment sessions** (one session with each partner) and then together for all the subsequent sessions unless there is a compelling reason to separate them due to emerging issues, volatility or other problems in the couple sessions.

The objective for you at this stage is to arrive at a conceptualization of the problems and how each individual views the issues in the relationship. Obviously, there is an emphasis on presenting problems, but in a CBT assessment there is also a focus on situations, emotions, behaviors and negative thoughts as well as on beliefs about the self, the partner and the relationship.

Initial Interview: Important Questions to Ask

Here is a list of fundamental background information that you will want to cover in your initial interview. You may already have your own checklist, but if not, this will give you basic data and ensure you won't miss anything:

- The length of time clients have known each other, been together as a couple, been married, or lived together
- Other relationships, marriages, divorces (this may be easier to do separately)
- Any periods of separation they have had
- Children's gender, ages, living at home or away, or step-children
- Jobs
- Family backgrounds
- Previous individual or couple therapy
- Any events/stressors they feel have contributed to the relationship problem
- Demands on the couple (individual and jointly)
- Resources and strengths (for example: patience, compassion, empathy)
- Factors which can prevent use of resources
- Relationship dynamics (changes in their relationship over time)

Beyond the basics, the initial intake continues with questions that delve into what has brought the couple to seek therapy. Below are questions that explore several important areas. In keeping with our integrative treatment perspective, you will notice that several of these questions use a Positive Psychology approach by focusing on positives and strengths.

1. Why do you want to stay together?
2. What are the positives in your relationship?
3. Why do you want to continue in this relationship (if you do)?
4. What are positive qualities/strengths which you bring to the relationship?
5. What are your partner's positive qualities/strengths which he/she brings to the relationship?
6. What attracted you to him/her initially?
7. What do you still find attractive/what positive qualities does he/she have?
8. How would you feel if you were not together/what would you miss or how much of a loss would this be to you?
9. What was good about your relationship when it was best?
10. What is good about your relationship now?
11. How hopeful are you that things can improve?

Note: These questions can be asked while the couple is interviewed together, but more honest responses may emerge if done with individuals alone or assigned for homework with instructions not to confer.

It is important to focus on positive aspects of the relationship, as well as the problems, and any motivation to change, in an effort to increase morale and engagement in couples who may be feeling demoralized.

It is also helpful to ask:

- Whose idea was it to get help with the relationship and why?
- What did the other partner think about this idea?

- What have you done together or individually to promote change?
- What could each of you do to improve the relationship?
- How much is each of you willing to work at creating change?

It is important to elicit mutual and collaborative goals for the couple for therapy, so it is important to ask:

- What changes do each of you want to see in the relationship?
- What is each of you willing to change?
- What would each of you like your partner to change?

Giving an early homework assignment, such as filling out any of the brief scales in this section, can help assess motivational factors and identify any defeatist beliefs. Filling out questionnaires as homework or engaging in a simple exercise together can be revealing in terms of the couple's ability to collaborate.

It may also be beneficial to ask questions about attempts to repair the relationship including previous counseling or self-directed efforts, and the outcome of those.

Contacting previous individual or couple therapists can be very helpful as a source of data especially if individual therapy for either partner is occurring at the same time. You should ask the clients to fill out the necessary releases to facilitate this.

ASSESSING AREAS OF CONFLICT OR PROBLEMS

Have you ever had a couple be vague or non-specific in their initial description of what is problematic in their relationship? That's not uncommon, and that's why it makes sense to have couples fill out a questionnaire in order to pinpoint issues.

The **Relationship Problems Questionnaire** can quickly identify specific areas to work on. There are several ways that you can introduce this questionnaire. For example, it can be given to the couple to complete while together in the first session, in individual assessment sessions or even as a homework assignment.

RELATIONSHIP PROBLEMS QUESTIONNAIRE

Please answer the following questions by rating how much of a problem or issue each of these is in your relationship at this time.

HOW MUCH OF A PROBLEM	0 NOT AT ALL	1 SOMEWHAT PROBLEMATIC	2 VERY PROBLEMATIC	3 EXTREMELY PROBLEMATIC
Finance				
Sex				
Demonstrations of affection				
Family				
Child rearing				
Friends				
Leisure pursuits				
Time together				
Arguments				
Values/goals				
Religion				
Household tasks				
Work or career				
Decision-making				
Communication				

Copyright 2018 © John W. Ludgate & Tereza N. Grubr, *The CBT Couples Toolbox*. All Rights Reserved

PSYCHOLOGICAL ISSUES

Also, it is important in the assessment phase to briefly assess individual psychopathology such as major depression, anxiety disorders, substance abuse or psychosis. A structured interview using psychometric instruments or other personality/ psychopathology measures can be conducted with one or both individuals.

If individual treatment is indicated, a decision can then be made about the sequencing of treatment. For example, issues like substance abuse or an acute, severe depressive episode may require treatment before the focus returns to couple therapy, as these disorders will impair the ability of individuals to benefit from or fully engage in couple therapy.

COMMUNICATION

Communication and the ability to listen is a vital skill that couples need to be successful. There are a couple tools to assess communication issues.

- Christensen (1988) describes a Communication Patterns Questionnaire which identifies destructive patterns like mutual attack, demand-withdrawal and mutual avoidance.

- Beck (1988) lists 42 issues commonly found in couples, which are presented in a questionnaire. These can be divided into four areas: making decisions, finance, sex relations and leisure activities.

We have created our own **Problems in Communication Questionnaire** that you can use to identify problems in communication and communication style. Have the couple each fill out this questionnaire separately. Afterwards, you can process in session with both partners how their communication is understood and perceived. This provides an ideal starting point for addressing communication issues and what needs changing.

PROBLEMS IN COMMUNICATION QUESTIONNAIRE

Rate each communication issue from 0-5 (0 = no problem, 5 = major problem).

COMMUNICATION ISSUE	YOUR PARTNER	WHAT YOUR PARTNER MIGHT SAY ABOUT YOU
Doesn't listen		
Talks too much/never gets to the point		
Avoids conflict		
Interrupts		
Nags		
Insists on being right		
Has to have last word		
Doesn't indicate agreement/ doesn't show interest		
Finds fault/criticizes frequently		
Gives advice too soon rather than listening		

Copyright 2018 © John W. Ludgate & Tereza N. Grubr, *The CBT Couples Toolbox*. All Rights Reserved

POSITIVES IN THE RELATIONSHIP

When integrating the more strengths-based assessment approach it is often helpful to assess positive behaviors as well as negative. In addition to the **Frequency of Positive Behaviors Questionnaire**, you might also want to consider the Beck (1998) Expressions of Love scale as a means of helping the couple recognize positives, or lack thereof, in their current relationship.

It can be revealing to ask each partner how they express their love and how they would like love expressed to them. This may reveal some discrepancies in how they want love to be expressed versus how it actually is expressed (more affectionate touch rather than a cursory peck on the cheek, spending time together rather than one partner working on the car).

You can also ask about the frequency and desirability of each of these and promote the idea that these behavioral expressions of love, when increased in frequency, are likely to lead to more marital happiness and satisfaction.

We have created a **Frequency of Positive Behaviors Questionnaire** on the next page that each partner can fill out separately. In processing this questionnaire with the couple, you will learn a lot about the importance of these behaviors and which ones are essential building blocks of feeling loved.

FREQUENCY OF POSITIVE BEHAVIORS QUESTIONNAIRE

How often do the following occur?

	NEVER	RARELY	OFTEN
Confiding in each other			
Physical affection, touching, kissing (non-sexual)			
Physical affection (sexual)			
Engaging in outside interests together			
Laughing together			
Working on a project together			
Going on a date			
Socializing with friends together			
Using terms of endearment			
Demonstrations of caring			
Missing partner when away			
Being careful to not say hurtful or critical things			

Copyright 2018 © John W. Ludgate & Tereza N. Grubr, *The CBT Couples Toolbox*. All Rights Reserved

BEHAVIORS

Assessment of behaviors can be done by self-report or questionnaires. You can also notice verbal and non-verbal behaviors when the clients are seen together and separately. Attention should be paid to destructive, manipulative, or aversive patterns in relating.

Sometimes couple therapists can set up a problem-solving scenario (Datillio, 2008) to observe how couples interact or how cooperative they are. How well couples tolerate frustrations with their partner or how they react to frustrations themselves can be very instructive. You can also observe in each partner:

- Assertiveness/unassertiveness
- Difficulty communicating clearly
- Problems in expressing self
- Difficulties listening
- Aversive control efforts
- Passive-aggressive behavior
- Controlling the partner

- Problem-solving skills deficits
- Overly reactive behaviors
- Poor conflict management skills
- Punitive style of interaction
- Intense, unregulated affect
- Poor reciprocity or negotiation skills

All of the assessment tools and questionnaires covered to this point should identify the couple's problem areas that need work. For other problems which may not have come up, you can use the following **Treatment Goals Checklist.** This checklist is useful if individuals are unable to articulate problems or have only focused on relationship issues and not focused on more personal issues such as those on this checklist.

TREATMENT GOALS
CHECKLIST

Think about your goals for therapy. It's different for everyone, so please check all that apply.

- ☐ Reduce a fear.
- ☐ Have more pleasurable activities.
- ☐ Improve communications with my: (circle) *Spouse / Children / Friends / Coworkers / Others*
- ☐ Express myself more assertively.
- ☐ Learn how to relax.
- ☐ Better manage my health.
- ☐ Better tolerate my mistakes.
- ☐ Better tolerate others' mistakes.
- ☐ Feel less guilt.
- ☐ Feel less depressed.
- ☐ Better accepting a loss/death.
- ☐ Increase my conversational skills.
- ☐ Learn how I come across to others.
- ☐ Not take disappointments so hard.
- ☐ Doubt myself less.
- ☐ Think more positively.
- ☐ Improve my sexual relationship.
- ☐ Control my eating or weight.
- ☐ Control my alcohol use.
- ☐ Change a habit.
- ☐ Control my drug use.
- ☐ Better manage my pain.
- ☐ Learn how to improve friendships.
- ☐ Reduce uncomfortable thoughts.
- ☐ Learn more effective parenting skills.

- ☐ Improve my sleep.
- ☐ Reduce my sensitivity to possible criticism.
- ☐ Talk out a pending decision.
- ☐ Problem-solving/decision-making techniques.
- ☐ Reduce panic attacks.
- ☐ Increase self-esteem.
- ☐ Reduce family difficulties.
- ☐ Reduce job difficulties.
- ☐ Better manage my temper.
- ☐ Take initiative more often.
- ☐ Receive medication help.
- ☐ Decrease procrastination.
- ☐ Better time management.
- ☐ Decrease trying to be perfect.
- ☐ Not reacting so emotionally.
- ☐ Allow myself to express my feelings more.
- ☐ Feel more self-confident.
- ☐ Discuss my thoughts of harming myself.
- ☐ Discuss my thoughts of harming others.
- ☐ Adjust better to a recent change/incident.
- ☐ Adjust better to a past incident.
- ☐ Become more optimistic.
- ☐ Improve my self-awareness.
- ☐ Adopt a healthier attitude.
- ☐ Worry less.

☐ Other (Specify) _____

_____

_____

_____

Copyright 2018 © John W. Ludgate & Tereza N. Grubr, *The CBT Couples Toolbox*. All Rights Reserved

Now please review your list and decide which three goals you would first want to discuss/change.

First _____

_____

_____

_____

_____

Second _____

_____

_____

_____

_____

Third _____

_____

_____

_____

_____

Copyright 2018 © John W. Ludgate & Tereza N. Grubr, *The CBT Couples Toolbox*. All Rights Reserved

CASE CONCEPTUALIZATION OF RELATIONSHIP PROBLEMS

Conceptualization or formulation is an important part of working with CBT or any allied therapies.

It helps to:
- Connect presenting problems and situations
- Increase your and the clients' understanding of the problem and its origins and maintenance
- Facilitate the strategic and logical use of interventions

There are two kinds of conceptualization to consider in your couples work: cross-sectional and longitudinal. Let's see how these compare and when they are useful.

Cross-sectional Conceptualization

This is generally done in conjunction with the initial assessment of problems. The steps involved are as follows:
- **Identify** a general problem
- **Pinpoint** a recent occurrence of the problem
- **Breakdown** the problem into the following components:
  - situational
  - feelings (emotional and physiological)
  - thoughts
  - behaviors

This involves asking the couple for the following information:
- What is one major problem in the relationship?
- Describe a time when it happened recently.

Focusing on this specific episode, ask about:
- **The situation** (What exactly happened?)
- **Feelings** (What did each person feel emotionally and in their body?)
- **Thoughts** (What thoughts did each partner have?)
- **Behaviors** (What did each person do?)

It may be best to start with one person's version of a problem and ask all of the questions of that individual before doing the same with the other, as sometimes the different versions will be disputed if both are simultaneously describing each stage and the analysis will be slowed down. The rationale can be given that it works better to have each describe what it was like for them in turn.

Here is an example of carrying out this exercise with one of the clients in a couple with relationship issues.
- **What is one major problem in the relationship?** *Him talking down to me, being insulting.*
- **Tell me about a time it happened recently.** *Last night he said there was a better way of organizing the children's homework. He said that they should do it earlier after they get back from school and I got mad and we didn't talk all night.*
- **Situation (What exactly happened?)** *He said "You should get them started on their homework when they get home from school rather than after dinner."*
- **Emotions (What did you feel?)** *Angry.*
- **Physiological (What happened in your body?)** *My face got flushed. My stomach was tight.*

- **Thoughts (What thoughts/images did you have?)** *He has no right to undermine what I am doing and talk down to me like this. I had the image of being a child and being scolded for doing something wrong.*
- **Behavior (What did you do or not do? What did your partner do or not do?)** *I went to the bedroom and stayed away from him. He kept trying to get me to talk about other things, asking what my day was like. I ignored him and didn't respond. He never apologized.*

At this point the partner would be asked exactly the same questions concerning his/her emotions, physiological feelings, thoughts and behaviors related to this problem situation.

Note: Each problem the clients report can be broken down in this way and new issues which emerge at any stage of couple treatment can be similarly dismantled.

After the couple have agreed on one problem to focus on, the therapist can use the **Cross-Sectional Concepualization** form on the next page to break down the problem into the components of the situations, emotions, physical feelings, thoughts and behaviors.

- What was the situation?
- What emotions did each partner have?
- What physical feelings did each partner have?
- What thoughts did each partner have?
- What behaviors did each partner engage in?

It will also be helpful to ask more general questions related to this problem area (not just focusing on the recent occurrence):

- How long has it been a problem?
- Have you had similar problems in the past?
- Why do you think it has become a problem?
- When does it occur most or when is it most severe?

Each problem the clients bring up in therapy can be broken down this way, and this will facilitate interventions. Here's an example of what a problem conceptualization worksheet might look like when completed:

	Problem 1: Arguing				
	Situation	**Emotions**	**Physical Feelings**	**Thoughts**	**Behaviors**
Client A	Dorothy wanted Dave to baby sit one night while she went out with her girlfriends. He said he didn't see why she wanted to go and they got in an argument.	(Dorothy) angry	(Dorothy) muscle tension, headache, stomach churning	(Dorothy) He always tries to control me. He doesn't care what I want. It's all about him.	(Dorothy) Yells. Tells him he is a selfish SOB. Criticizes his friends and compares them unfavorably to hers. Has several drinks.
Client B	Dave was annoyed that Dorothy wanted to go out.	(Dave) anxious, irritated	(Dave) face red, chest tightness	(Dave) She enjoys their company more than mine. She should be there for me after the hard days I put in at work.	(Dave) Withdraws. Ignores her. Takes children outside and plays with them. Goes to sleep early without her.

CROSS-SECTIONAL CONCEPTUALIZATION

	Problem 1:				
	Situation	Emotions	Physical Feelings	Thoughts	Behaviors
Client A					
Client B					

Copyright 2018 © John W. Ludgate & Tereza N. Grubr, *The CBT Couples Toolbox*. All Rights Reserved

Having completed these steps, it is important to then come up with a plan.

1. **Identify treatment goals or targets.** (What do both partners want to change?)

   In the example, both Dorothy and Dave indicated they wished to stop the arguments and be able to resolve issues without negative feelings. It should be noted that in some high conflict couples it could be hard to get them to agree on a goal. If so, some additional work will need to be done on facilitating a collaborative mindset and establishing mutual goals which are in both of their best interests.

2. **Select interventions** connected to the goal. (What techniques will be most likely used to achieve the target?)

   For the previous example, the therapist selected communication training, conflict resolution, modifying cognitive distortions in both partners (her assumption of control, his assumption that she preferred her friends' company to his) and altering behaviors (withdrawal, passive aggression on his part and yelling and counterattack on hers).

Below are some things to watch for when using cross-sectional conceptualization in couple therapy. You can address and clarify any of these issues should they occur.

- The problem is too vague and there is not enough specificity.
- There is a difficulty in dismantling problems in the way described previously.
- Clients have problems in identifying thoughts or feelings.
- The targets selected by each are different or incompatible.
- The interventions you choose are not tied strategically to the targets and are applied in a mechanical way.

Longitudinal Conceptualization

When you know the couple better, you may attempt to formulate an opinion by looking at their history and what predisposes each individual to act and think as they do in their relationship interactions. This is called longitudinal case formulation. This diagram shows how, using a CBT perspective, you can conduct this type of formulation.

RELEVANT CHILDHOOD OR OTHER FORMATIVE EVENTS
(What key events happened to the client
which relate to relationship beliefs?)

CORE BELIEFS DEVELOPED
(What beliefs did this client come to hold?)

TRIGGERS
(What current relationship events trigger these beliefs?)

AUTOMATIC THOUGHTS
(What thoughts did the client have related to this situation?)

EMOTIONS
(What emotions or feelings are involved?)

PHYSIOLOGIC RESPONSES
(How did the client's body react?)

BEHAVIORS
(What did the client do?)

Longitudinal formulation helps explore the origins and maintenance of some relationship issues. Below is an example of what this formulation could look like after careful questioning of the client (in the individual assessment session or later).

RELEVANT CHILDHOOD OR OTHER FORMATIVE EVENTS
(What key events happened to the client
which relate to relationship beliefs?)

Observed parents never arguing and was aware that
uncle and aunt who fought publicly ended up divorced.

CORE BELIEFS DEVELOPED
(What beliefs did this client come to hold?)

Partners should never argue. If they do, their relationship will fail.

TRIGGERS
(What current relationship events trigger these beliefs?)

Mild argument or difference of opinion with spouse.

AUTOMATIC THOUGHTS
(What thoughts did the client have related to this situation?)

This is terrible. We will end up apart.

EMOTIONS
(What emotions or feelings are involved?)

Anxiety

PHYSIOLOGIC RESPONSES
(How did the client's body react?)

Nervous stomach, palpitations, appetite loss, physical tension

BEHAVIORS
(What did the client do?)

Tells spouse they have to agree and can't have
difference of opinion. Insists partner change opinion or
alternately decides to completely give in, but continues
to be resentful about issues that came up in the argument.

It is clear in this example that the underlying beliefs need to be explored and tested out rather than making a more superficial attempt to create conflict resolution. The beliefs that any disagreement or conflict is bad and must be suppressed at all costs creates a vulnerability to relationship distress which is likely to re-emerge. This approach explores other beliefs clients have about themselves, their partner or other people: "I will be rejected," "People cannot be trusted," or "My partner is stronger and more powerful than me." These beliefs need to be challenged and modified during therapy as they have the potential to interfere with functioning interpersonally and within the relationship.

At this point also, family of origin beliefs relevant to each partner may emerge which can be in conflict. For example, clients Alberto and Deborah, who had very different views about the raising of voices, came to realize through the therapist sharing his formulation that in their upbringing (his in Italy, hers in the Mid-West) raised voices had very different meanings. With this new understanding and using some role reversal exercises, they learned to be less attached to their own viewpoint and to see things from each other's perspective.

Three Levels of Cognition

In the context of CBT, there are three levels of cognition. These are relevant in the assessment and conceptualization phase for each individual. While these will be discussed in more detail in Chapter 4, they play an important role during the formulation stage.

- **Negative Automatic Thoughts:** These are specific thoughts or images related to specific situations such as, "She is mad at me" or "I am stupid."

- **Cognitive Distortions:** This refers to errors in thinking or thinking style which are influenced by beliefs and create upset. Examples are black or white thinking, overgeneralizing and mind reading.

- **Beliefs:** These are general assumptions or ways of looking at the world, oneself and others by which experiences are viewed and interpreted such as, "I am incompetent," "No one can be trusted," or "Relationships are very risky."

Define negative automatic thoughts: The negative automatic thoughts and distortions found when clients are upset will be tracked throughout therapy as situations come up. Later in therapy, the distortions and the belief systems of each partner and how they impact the relationship will be explored.

You can take a problem and ask what exactly the thoughts are when each partner is upset in this situation and identify what emotions are felt. Having demonstrated this in session, you can help clients practice this during real-world situations. This is accomplished by having both clients keep a small notebook or use their phone to write down thoughts and feelings whenever issues arise. Or, they can simply fill out the form on page 44 as a homework assignment.

To elicit cognitive distortions, identify which cognitive errors are operative for the couple. Once couples learn to recognize their own distortions, they can also make note of these should they occur during moments of reactivity.

Additionally, in the initial interview it is important to have a preliminary assessment of the couple's beliefs about each other, their relationship and relationships in general. Assessing beliefs about relationships is a vital part of any CBT assessment of couple problems, as relationship beliefs can have a tremendous influence on efforts to change and optimism/hope regarding this.

We've created two questionnaires, **Beliefs Impacting Change** and **Attitude About Relationships** that will help you to expose and pinpoint beliefs the couple holds. Once completed, you can assess these beliefs for each partner, as well as investigate the impact such beliefs have on the relationship.

BELIEFS IMPACTING CHANGE

Please indicate how much you believe any of the statements below. Please be honest about how you feel.

	NOT AT ALL	A LITTLE	QUITE A BIT	A LOT
My partner is incapable of change.				
I cannot change.				
Our relationship has been bad for too long to change it now.				
I won't change until he/she does.				
I won't make an effort if she/he won't.				
My partner is not interested in changing/doesn't care enough about me or us.				
If we talk about our relationship, it will get worse not better, as it will open up stuff best forgotten or ignored.				
It won't matter if he/she changes behaviors, it is the feelings and attitude that won't change.				
I don't feel any of it is my fault; he/she needs to change.				
My partner has serious problems that are responsible for our issues.				
This only postpones the inevitable, which is us splitting up.				
Since he/she hurt me, he/she deserves to be punished or suffer.				

Copyright 2018 © John W. Ludgate & Tereza N. Grubr, *The CBT Couples Toolbox*. All Rights Reserved

ATTITUDE ABOUT RELATIONSHIPS

Think about your relationship. How much do you believe each of these statements?

BELIEF	NOT AT ALL	A LITTLE	QUITE A BIT	A LOT
Quarrels should not happen.				
My partner being critical means he/she doesn't love me.				
He/she should know what I need without me saying.				
If he/she cared, they would always do what I want.				
Hurting my feelings or upsetting me is always deliberate.				
A good relationship has no problems.				
My partner is incapable of change.				

Copyright 2018 © John W. Ludgate & Tereza N. Grubr, *The CBT Couples Toolbox*. All Rights Reserved

SHARING THE FORMULATION

Turning problems into goals may take up much of the first several sessions, but it is critical to have specific targets to create meaningful change.

After developing a conceptualization and treatment plan, give the couple feedback in the session when they come back together (usually in session 4) about the formulation and results of the assessment. At this point their feedback is elicited, a plan of action proposed and a treatment contract initiated. The conceptualization should be shared in simple, non-technical terms and their individual responses noted. Hopefully, there will be "buy in" at this point and, if not, a discussion can ensue about how each partner sees things if it is different from the conceptualization.

This formulation should focus on strengths, as well as problems, and also on those factors which impinge on the relationship, such as life demands and stressors. Constructive actions the clients have already taken need to be reinforced, in addition to problem identification.

TREATMENT PLAN

Now you and the couple can begin to develop a written treatment plan stating the couple's goals, objectives and the treatment approach.

Effective treatment goals are specific, achievable and measurable. A copy of the treatment plan should be given to each partner. With the tools in this chapter, you will be well on your way to a solid case formulation, assessing a couple's needs, and providing a well thought out treatment plan for working with them.

We'll conclude this chapter with an example of a couple-oriented treatment plan. We've also provided a blank **Treatment Plan** form for you to use with clients.

SAMPLE TREATMENT PLAN
BILLY AND FRIEDA

IDENTIFIED PROBLEM	GOAL	SPECIFIC STEPS TO ACHIEVE GOAL
Arguing	Resolve conflict in a healthy way	Validation of the other's feelings. Assertion without raising voice. Good listening skills.
Not spending time together	Increase time spent together without other focus (kids, phone)	Schedule 1 date night per week. Put aside 2 hours on weekends for "hanging out".
In-law conflict	Acceptance of Billy's family	Plan out together when family will visit and how to spend time. Frieda to reduce critical comments about her in-laws.
Inequality re: child-rearing responsibilities	Develop more reciprocity or sharing of duties	Billy to help out with kids' activities on weekends. Make plan each week for who will put kids to bed or supervise homework each day.

Copyright 2018 © John W. Ludgate & Tereza N. Grubr, *The CBT Couples Toolbox*. All Rights Reserved

Treatment Plan

Names:

IDENTIFIED PROBLEM	GOAL	SPECIFIC STEPS TO ACHIEVE GOAL

Copyright 2018 © John W. Ludgate & Tereza N. Grubr, *The CBT Couples Toolbox*. All Rights Reserved

CHAPTER 2:
Client Engagement

Client engagement in therapy is an issue we all deal with. A major development in fostering motivation for change and engagement in therapy has been the introduction of Motivational Interviewing (Miller & Rollnick, 2013), which can be used to augment Cognitive Behavior Therapy and other therapy approaches. In couples therapy, Motivational Interviewing strategies can be used with good effect to facilitate change. This chapter will outline specific procedures for fostering engagement. Initially, Motivational Interviewing was introduced in the field of substance abuse because the existing models had not been found to be effective in terms of longer term positive outcome. Subsequently, Motivational Interviewing has been shown to be effective in many studies (Arkowitz, Miller & Rollnick, 2015) and has been applied in the fields of anxiety, depression, habit change, medical compliance and other areas, in addition to its original use in substance abuse.

Let's examine some of the key characteristics and benefits of Motivational Interviewing:
- It is non-confrontational and non-judgmental
- It involves validation, compassion and empathy
- It is collaborative and involves a "guided discovery" approach
- It explores clients' perceptions about change and the need to change
- It supports self-efficacy (not just that an individual should change but also can change)

In addition, it reinforces change talk, "rolls with" ambivalence about change, reinforces strengths and assets, and crucially develops a discrepancy between the cost and benefits of change and those of maintaining the status quo, which can motivate individuals. And it offers a mindfulness-oriented, non-judging and compassionate style that helps clients feel accepted and fosters a greater therapeutic alliance.

MEASURING MOTIVATION

In addition to engaging clients through Motivational Interviewing, it is important to assess where clients stand in regards to motivation. This can be done using the stages of change model proposed by Prochaska & DiClemente (1984).

The five stages in the change process are:

- **Pre-contemplation**
  Clients may feel that nothing is wrong; they do not have a problem or need to change.

- **Contemplation**
  Clients are likely to be ambivalent, feeling they may have a problem or need to change, but are unsure about why they need to change or about their ability to change.

- **Preparation**
  Clients will have decided that they have a problem and need to change. They are often considering what to do to solve the problem and may start thinking of a plan.

- **Action**
  Clients are becoming active in making changes and working on problems. By themselves or with others they make a plan for making changes that they can start acting on.

- **Maintenance**
  Clients are maintaining changes made and sustaining their efforts. This stage also recognizes that relapse or return to old habits is possible and works to prevent that.

It is important to note that clients coming for counseling may be at any stage in the change sequence. This is also true of working with couples where ideally each partner or the couple should be at the preparation stage but often are at the following stages:

- **Pre-contemplation** (each believing he/she does not have a problem, only the other partner does, or that the relationship is fine).
- **Contemplation** (not really sure if the relationship is problematic and if what they are experiencing in their relationship is an issue).

Importantly, partners can be at different stages. For example, one is in the preparation or action stage (recognizes a problem and is ready to work on it) while the other may be pre-contemplation or contemplation, as described above.

You should not assume that clients (an individual or a couple) are showing up in your office ready to start working on effecting change. In couples therapy, one partner may be "mandated" to be there ("either you come to therapy or else") or may believe that they themselves are not the problem but rather the other partner is totally responsible for their issues since that partner has been unfaithful or has substance abuse issues, for example.

A careful assessment of motivation Zuckoff (2015) provides helpful tools. On the following page is the **Need for Change Questionnaire** which can be utilized early in couples' treatment, preferably during the assessment phase. This would ideally be administered to each person separately so there is no fear of negative reactions on the part of their partner to responses made honestly.

NEED FOR CHANGE QUESTIONNAIRE

Please indicate **honestly** which of the statements below best describes your attitude toward, or feeling about, making this change in your life at this time.

☐ I don't need to make changes. Nothing is wrong.

☐ Maybe I need to make changes but I am uncertain.

☐ I need to make changes and am considering how to.

☐ I have started making some changes.

☐ I am keeping the changes I have made going.

If you have any comments or wish to elaborate on what you answered above, please use the space below.

_____

_____

_____

_____

_____

_____

_____

_____

Copyright 2018 © John W. Ludgate & Tereza N. Grubr, *The CBT Couples Toolbox*. All Rights Reserved

The goal of therapy is to help clients move from pre-contemplation, contemplation and preparation to action and maintenance. But commonly clients don't progress through these stages in a straight line, but instead may revert to an earlier stage owing to discouragement, new issues coming up that make change difficult or feeling worse rather than better. You then need to assess what has changed in the motivational picture in an open, non-confrontational manner aimed at conceptualizing the changeover. Once you understand where someone is on the stages of changes model, you can use Motivational Interviewing to validate clients in a non-confrontational way that helps them explore new change strategies.

For example, George and Ivy were making some changes in their patterns of communication and being more accepting of each other after five sessions of couple therapy when they announced that they wanted to discontinue therapy. They justified this decision by saying they felt their relationship really was never that bad to start with and not in need of change. Careful, non-judgmental probing by the therapist revealed that they both felt overwhelmed by the various exercises they were doing to improve the relationship, given other demands (job, family) in their lives. The therapist collaboratively discussed with them some ways of dealing with those issues.

In assessing motivation it is important to evaluate these three dimensions:

- Are the clients **willing?** (Have they both made a commitment to change?)
- Are the clients **ready?** (Are they both ready to be active behaviorally in changing?)
- Do the clients perceive themselves to be **capable of change?** (Do they each have a sense of self-efficacy or confidence that they or their relationship can change?)

These are often described as the three legs of the motivation stool. Each needs to be carefully assessed and, unless each is in place, sustained change is unlikely.

As an example of this, consider John and Julie, a couple who realized they had "drifted a long way apart" and needed to work on their relationship. During a family get-together when they observed the intimacy between Julie's brother and his wife, they talked about rekindling their own relationship. They committed to each other and to a course of therapy (they were willing). However, they found it hard to be engaged in the exercises suggested by the therapist due to two factors:

1. Not being able to make enough time in their busy lives for their relationship (a readiness issue).
2. John's belief that they could not rescue their relationship as they had been like this for too long (self-efficacy issue).

Although on the surface this couple seemed very motivated, it was important that the therapist addressed these issues to improve the chances of a positive outcome. These two factors may need to be assessed separately for each partner. It may also be helpful to ask each partner to predict how the other partner is likely to fill out some of the motivational questions on page 30 as these beliefs ("My partner isn't committed to change," or "My partner won't actually do anything to make change happen") will be stumbling blocks to therapy if not addressed.

It is also important for you to pay attention to statements clients make during discussions in the early and later stages of therapy regarding change. In particular, it is helpful to look for "change talk" and "sustain talk." Motivational interviewers describe "change talk" as any indication the client is aware of the need to make changes or that the client is keen to alter a situation or behavior, while "sustain talk" is anything the client says which supports the status quo (no change).

In their statements regarding their relationship during the assessment (and therapy) the therapist may hear a mixture of both change and sustain talk in clients. For example, a client might say, "I really wish we could be as close as we used to be and I really want us to spend more time together and be more intimate (change talk), but I think we have been this way now for so long it probably won't change and I don't think I want to put in a lot of effort if she doesn't value that (sustain talk)." This suggests some ambivalent motivation and can be the subject for a discussion about the costs and benefits of change.

The three forms on the following pages, **Feelings About Change Questionnaire**, **No Change/Continuing as We Are in Our Relationship** and **Changing Our Relationship in Ways Discussed with the Therapist**, can serve as a springboard for discussion regarding the couple's feelings about the pros and cons of change. Ask each member of the couple to fill them out independently, then share and discuss them in future sessions.

FEELINGS ABOUT CHANGE QUESTIONNAIRE

Please answer the following questions.

How committed am I to change (0-10)? _____

How committed do I believe my partner is to change (0-10)? _____

Explain the ratings above, if necessary: _____

_____

_____

_____

How ready am I to be active in doing specific things to create change (0-10)? _____

How ready do I believe my partner is to be active in doing specific things to create change (0-10)? _____

Explain the ratings above, if necessary: _____

_____

_____

_____

How much confidence do I have that I, my partner or our relationship can change (0-10)?

_____

How much confidence do I believe my partner has that he/she, I or our relationship can change (0-10)?

_____

Explain the ratings above, if necessary: _____

_____

_____

_____

_____

_____

Copyright 2018 © John W. Ludgate & Tereza N. Grubr, *The CBT Couples Toolbox.* All Rights Reserved

No Change/Continuing as We Are in Our Relationship

BENEFITS What is good or will be good about this?	COSTS What is or will be bad about this?

Once completed go back over the items on each side and indicate with an * or other symbol those which are especially important to you.

Copyright 2018 © John W. Ludgate & Tereza N. Grubr, *The CBT Couples Toolbox.* All Rights Reserved

CHANGING OUR RELATIONSHIP IN WAYS DISCUSSED WITH THE THERAPIST

BENEFITS What do I /we stand to gain? What would be the advantages or upside?	COSTS What would be hard? What would be the disadvantages or downside?

Once completed go back over the items on each side and indicate with an * or other symbol those which are especially important to you.

Copyright 2018 © John W. Ludgate & Tereza N. Grubr, *The CBT Couples Toolbox.* All Rights Reserved

When the couple sees that the benefits of change outweigh its costs, motivation to change increases. Also, when some of these are highly valued (rated as being important on the list) it can propel clients forward to change. (Alternately, when they view the costs of continuing "as is" outweighing the benefits, motivation to change can be hindered.)

GROUND RULES FOR THERAPY

During this early stage of therapy, the ground rules for therapy will be outlined. This is both an attempt to socialize clients to couple therapy and an engagement strategy. It's important to establish these ground rules to guide the partners' behavior during the therapy. You should talk about any issues the couple may have with these as they may represent motivational blocks or interfere with therapy.

On the following page is an example of some ground rules that we find useful in our practices.

GROUND RULES FOR THERAPY

• The relationship is the focus, not the individual.

• The couple agree with the concept of shared responsibility for problems experienced.

• The focus will be on building up positive behavior and on translating complaints to requests.

• Individuals are encouraged to refrain from scapegoating/blaming or being derogatory or hostile to the partner.

• The therapist will not "take sides."

• There will not be collateral contacts with individuals in between sessions unless there is an emergency.

• There will be a respect for each individual's privacy where homework is to be done separately.

• In the event of serious conflict, rage or anger occurring within the session, the following steps will be taken:

_____

_____

_____

_____

• In the event of violence or abuse, the following steps will be taken:

_____

_____

_____

_____

Copyright 2018 © John W. Ludgate & Tereza N. Grubr, *The CBT Couples Toolbox.* All Rights Reserved

CHAPTER 3:
Cognitive Behavioral
Therapy (CBT) Strategies

Before using any therapy approach you'll want to help your clients understand it better and see how it can work for them. Therefore, educating the clients about CBT is an essential first step in using this form of therapy with couples. It typically takes place during the first or second session and is an important part of treatment planning.

Key points of CBT to teach your clients:

1. CBT shows how there is a relationship between thoughts, feelings and behavior.
2. CBT shows how thought distortions and beliefs play a role in creating emotional and behavioral disturbance.
3. CBT will help clients learn to identify and challenge their thinking patterns.
4. The way in which CBT-based therapy will proceed, including your role and the role of each client.

Methods of educating clients:

1. Inquire if clients know anything about CBT from personal experience, friends and family, or media. If so discuss what is known, and correct any misconceptions.
2. Describe the model verbally or in diagram form.

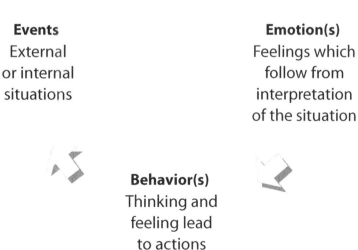

Thoughts
Meaning or
interpretation
of situation

Events
External
or internal
situations

Emotion(s)
Feelings which
follow from
interpretation
of the situation

Behavior(s)
Thinking and
feeling lead
to actions

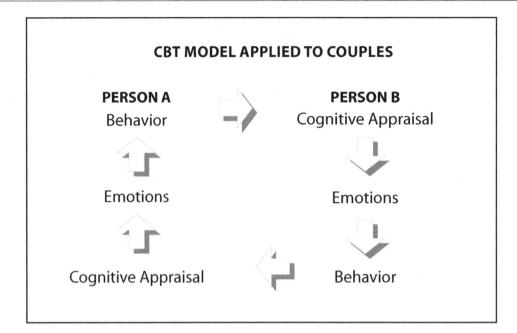

3. Reading materials can be helpful aids in describing the model. Sections of *Love is Never Enough* (Beck, 1988), *Feeling Good Together* (Burns, 2008) or other written descriptions can be utilized as a method of introducing this model as it applies to couples. It is important that these readings be brief and easily understood to facilitate both compliance with the reading assignment and understanding. Adequate time should be allotted to answer any questions or clear up any confusion which may arise in completing reading assignments.

4. Examples, anecdotes and cartoons can also be used to illustrate the model. A cartoon or anecdote can help clients understand the powerful effects which interpretations and appraisals can have on emotional reactions.

5. You might want to demonstrate the model using a problem the clients are currently experiencing. This might better help them to grasp the connection between how their partner's behavior directly affects their own thoughts, feelings and subsequent behavior. For example:

   • Partner's behavior: The wife says, "I could use some help getting the kids to bed."

   • Other partner's thoughts: "She has no right to get at me for not doing what is her job since I work hard all day."

   • Other partner's emotions: Irritation.

   • Other partner's behavior: Storms off and goes to another room.

What clients can expect with CBT:

1. Give the couple a brief handout explaining what this therapy is and how it will be helpful (on page 39).

2. Explain and give a rationale for the following:
   • structuring sessions
   • the collaborative/team approach
   • the importance of homework and practice in CBT

3. Check the reactions to the reading by asking clients, "How suitable do you feel this kind of therapy is to your problems?" "Do you have any points of disagreement with this approach?"

A GUIDE TO COGNITIVE BEHAVIOR THERAPY

Cognitive Behavior Therapy (CBT) is a form of short-term, problem-focused therapy which has been successfully used with several psychological and emotional problems, including depression, anxiety and addictive behaviors, over the last 20-30 years. In recent years, CBT has also been applied to relationship issues with research showing its effectiveness.

CBT aims to help clients identify and change thinking and behavior patterns which cause distress.

The CBT approach suggests that:

- Thoughts play a major role in the emotional and behavioral problems experienced by individuals. While situations (a friend not returning a telephone call) can elicit some feelings (irritation or anxiety), the way we think about this situation ("Something is wrong" or "This person doesn't care") can make the emotional reaction more severe or intense.

- Behaviors can also be part of the problem. For example, if the individual, who is feeling bad waiting for a call from a friend, calls repeatedly leaving angry messages for the other person, it is likely the situation will be made worse.

- Exploring the connection between situations, thoughts, feelings and behavior will be helpful in revealing maladaptive thinking or behavioral patterns which can then be changed leading to less emotional distress.

CBT therapy sessions tend to be:

- Structured (there is a clear plan for each session)
- Focused largely on present problems which are causing distress
- Collaborative (client and therapist work together to find solutions)
- Skill-building (clients learn skills which can help to deal better with problem situations and practice these both within and between sessions)
- Emphasize thinking and behavior patterns which may be more effective than those in operation currently

CBT applied to couples:

- Identifies thinking styles behind couples' perceptions of each other
- Looks at underlying beliefs about the relationship and each other
- Examines the interactional patterns which cause distress
- Focuses on practical ways to change all the above

Copyright 2018 © John W. Ludgate & Tereza N. Grubr, *The CBT Couples Toolbox*. All Rights Reserved

CBT will look at areas of dissatisfaction within the relationship from each partner's perspective and look at factors that contribute to this lack of satisfaction (partner's behavior, unrealistic expectations, external stressors) and attempt to modify these.

Some goals of CBT may be to alter unrealistic expectations of each other ("He should know what I need without me asking," "She should want intimacy whenever I do"), correct wrong attributions for each other's behaviors ("He\she meant to hurt me by saying something negative about my parents") and end destructive exchanges (the use of sarcasm, contempt, withdrawal during conflict).There may also be an emphasis on increasing positive behaviors (acts of affection or caring) and expressions of gratitude.

Techniques which may be used include:

- Evidence review (Is there a good reason to believe what is assumed?)
- Generating alternatives (Is there another way one could look at this?)
- Reviewing the usefulness of thoughts (Does it help to think this way?)
- Decatastrophizing (How likely is it that something bad will happen and what could be done if it did?)
- Action plan (What can be done to check things out or to improve the situation?)

These strategies will be explained in greater detail and practiced during CBT sessions, which generally will be with the couple together. In the early assessment phase the couples may see the therapist on their own to give information but otherwise all sessions will be together.

During each session, similar to individual CBT, there will be a plan or agenda when one or two problems will be focused on, discussion and identification of the problem related to the current issues will proceed systematically, possible solutions will be considered and then selected, and the therapist, in collaboration with the couple, may assign homework for the partners to work on in the intervening period until the next session. Feedback regarding the session, and the therapy in general, will also be sought in a systematic way and any issues arising will be discussed.

The aim is for the couple to ultimately become their own therapist using the improved relationship skills on their own in between sessions and after CBT, which is usually short term, ends.

Copyright 2018 © John W. Ludgate & Tereza N. Grubr, *The CBT Couples Toolbox*. All Rights Reserved

CONDUCTING A COGNITIVE BEHAVIOR THERAPY SESSION

Whether you and the couple are meeting for a regular, scheduled session, are having an informal "check-in," or are having a session precipitated by a crisis, the following guidelines for effectively structuring the session or interchange will probably make the session more productive and beneficial. These questions can be addressed to both partners simultaneously or individually. Below is a typical session outline that provides structure for clients that is clear, direct and collaborative.

Session outline

1. **Review the clients' concerns and the current state of the relationship:** (a general inquiry focusing on both partners to set up the agenda)

   "What's been on your mind recently?"

   "How have you been doing together since we last talked?"

   "How has your relationship been generally?"

   "How has your problem been?"

   "Has anything happened to upset you recently?"

2. **Feedback on last session/therapy:** (to elicit other agenda items)

   "Did you have any thoughts about our last session?"

   "Do you have any concerns about your therapy?"

3. **Set agenda:** (using information from 1 and 2 above)

   "What would you like to talk about today?"

   "What is on our agenda for today?"

   "What problems should we work on this session?"

4. **Review homework:** (this should always be one of the first items on the agenda to show how important homework is)

   "How did the homework go/any problems?"

   "What have you learned?"

   "How could you follow up on this?"

5. **Today's problems:** (working systematically through items on the agenda)

   "What exactly is the problem?"

   "In what situation does it occur?"

   "Can you give a recent example?"

   "What exactly happened?"

   "What feelings did you have?"

   "What thoughts did you have?"

   "Can you see how the situation's thoughts and feelings connect?"

6. **Homework assignment:** (try to collaboratively come up with an assignment to continue the work done in this session or elsewhere)

   "What could you do to work some more on this issue?"

   "Is there anything you can think of that might follow up on today's discussion?"

If clients cannot come up with anything, make a suggestion but then ask:

"How does this sound?"

"Would it be helpful, do you think?"

"Is there anything you don't understand concerning why you are doing this or what exactly you will do?"

"Do you anticipate any difficulties?"/ "If so, what could become a problem or an obstacle?"

7. **Summary and feedback:** (at the end of the session)

"What were the main things we discussed today?"

"What did we decide to do for homework and why?"

"What conclusions did we come to?"

"What, if anything, did you learn in today's session?"

"Is there anything you are unclear about or don't understand?"

If the clients cannot summarize or abstract the main points and the homework, do it for them and ask for feedback regarding whether they understand or are confused. It sometimes helps to have clients write down the main points, plus their homework, or listen to a tape of their session later to remind them. You can also write down key things to be remembered and give it to clients to take away.

"How did you feel about today's session/discussion?"

"What was this session like for you?"

"Was it helpful?" / "If so, anything in particular?"

"Was there anything unhelpful or upsetting?"

"Did I do anything which you didn't like or had any negative reaction to?"

If any negative feedback is given, it is important to address this, discuss it openly in the moment or schedule time to do so in the next session or some other time. "How are you feeling now?" If any positive change, follow up with: "Why do you think you feel differently/better?"

HELPING CLIENTS IDENTIFY THOUGHTS, BELIEFS AND DISTORTIONS

Conduct a cognitive analysis of conflict

Assessing the specific components involved in an episode of conflict can be done using these methods:

Focus on a problem one or both experienced

Steps:
1. Identify, in general terms, the nature of the problem.
2. Find a recent example: "When did this problem last bother you?"
3. Identify the situation: "What exactly happened?"
4. Identify the feeling: "What did you feel?" "How bad was the feeling(s) (0-100)?"
5. Identify thoughts. "What exactly were you thinking when in this situation or as you started to feel bad?"
6. Search for other thoughts: "What other thoughts, if any, did you have?"

Note: The question should be phrased "What thoughts did you have?" not "Were you having any thoughts?" It is also very important to use the client's own words when writing down or further discussing these thoughts.

Focus on a distressing emotion one or both experienced

Steps:
1. Identify the distressing emotion: "How exactly were you feeling last night when you said you got upset?" "How bad was the feeling(s) (0-100)?"
2. Identify the situation the client was in when the emotional shift occurred: "When exactly did the feeling start?" "What were you doing?" "What was going on?"
3. Identify thoughts: "What exactly were you thinking when you started to feel bad/anxious?"
4. Look for other thoughts (as in above). Try to find a thought strong enough to account for the level of emotion experienced. Ask yourself whether you would feel this bad if you had such a thought.

Here are some ways of dealing with problems, identifying thoughts:

- If clients have a hard time recalling either the feelings or thoughts they experienced in the recent or more distant past, it may help to ask them to imagine it happening in the present using **imagery.**

  Example: "Imagine you are there right now. Close your eyes and hear your partner criticizing you. Tell me what you feel now? What are you thinking now?"

- If the clients have no obvious thoughts, ask what was the **significance** or **meaning** of the situation.

  Example: "You don't remember having any thoughts then but what did it mean to you that you were watching TV just the two of you last Saturday night?"

- If clients do not report any thoughts, ask them if they were aware of any **images**, **mental pictures**, or **memories** passing through their minds at these times when upset. Educate them regarding what images are.

- Give clients examples of automatic thoughts in case they are not sure what you mean by these terms. Describe them as "what you say to yourself" or any other term which clarifies the meaning.

Mood shift in session

Inquire into the cognitions involved in any mood shift you observe in the session (from either verbal or non-verbal behavior or other observations).

Example: "You look sad/angry right now. What exactly are you feeling? What is passing through your mind at this moment? What thoughts are you having just now?"

Identify thoughts and feelings

As a problem is being discussed you can write down, either on a whiteboard or on the worksheet **Identifying Thoughts and Feelings,** the relevant thoughts, feelings and behaviors involved in this problem situation. Showing clients the sequence of **events->thoughts->feelings->behaviors** in black and white helps enormously to dismantle the problem and demonstrate how the CBT model applies. This procedure also models what they can do as a homework assignment.

For example, Sam and Betty had an unpleasant exchange related to Betty initiating sex and being "turned down" by Sam. The therapist asked each a series of questions (What was the situation for you, what were you thinking, what were you feeling and what did you do) and then wrote down their responses on the sample worksheet (page 43).

Clearly demonstrating and practicing this in session first, helps to model what your clients will be doing on their own as homework and maximizes the chances of success. Following the use of this method in therapy sessions, the clients should be given a copy of the **Identifying Thoughts and Feelings** worksheet and encouraged (as soon as they are able to do this) to work on identifying and recording their negative thoughts on their own when they next experience distress in their relationship.

The homework assignment can be set up as follows:

- **Starting with a shift in emotion**
  "The next time either of you starts to feel upset, I want you to write down exactly how you felt and how severe it was, what situation you were in, and what thoughts you had."
  The patient can do this using the form found on page 44.

- **Starting with a problem situation or thoughts**
  "You can do exactly the same thing (using the three steps on page 46) when in the situations that give you trouble or when you become aware of any of those thoughts (e.g. self-criticism, perfectionism, fear of rejection, unfairness) which we found were characteristic negative thoughts for you."

- **Rationale for writing down thoughts**
  "When we are upset we have many thoughts rushing through our minds. By writing them down, we slow up the process. We can look a little more objectively at these thoughts, which may help us to feel better by giving us some distance and, most importantly, give us an accurate record of our "hot" thoughts to allow us to work on these in therapy later on. The next step is going to be helping you to modify these thoughts so we need to know exactly what they are at this point. If we rely on our memories of the thoughts, the chances are that after a period of time, what we recall will be a bit different from exactly what we thought back when we were upset. For these reasons, you should try to write down your thoughts and feelings either while in the situation or while you are feeling upset or, if this is not feasible, at the very next available opportunity. Does this make sense? Do you have any questions about this?"

Sam

Situation

Betty initiated sexual activity

Thought

Doesn't she know how hard I worked and how tired I am?

Feeling

Irritation

Behavior

Removed her hand and turned away in bed

Betty

Situation

Sam pushes my hand away and turns away from me

Thought

He doesn't find me attractive anymore

Feeling

Sad
Hurt

Behavior

Cries silently in bed

IDENTIFYING THOUGHTS AND FEELINGS

When you experience strong emotions or are experiencing a problem related to your relationship try to write down, as soon as you can, each of the components of your conflict on this form.

Name

_____

Situation

_____
_____
_____

Thought

_____
_____
_____

Feeling

_____
_____
_____

Name

_____

Behavior

_____
_____

Situation

_____
_____
_____

Feeling

_____
_____

Thought

_____
_____
_____

Behavior

_____
_____
_____

Copyright 2018 © John W. Ludgate & Tereza N. Grubr, *The CBT Couples Toolbox*. All Rights Reserved

- **Summarizing seeking feedback and problem-solving any anticipated difficulties**

"To make sure you understand this homework assignment, let's just review what's involved. What exactly are you going to do? What is the purpose of doing this? Is there anything not clear about this? Do you anticipate any difficulties with this?"

Possible issues which may emerge for the clients at this stage might include:

- Anticipating not having enough time to do homework (you and the clients need to reset priorities)

- Anticipating failure or predicting that you might be displeased (you need to set it up as a no-fail task and also examine the evidence for this prediction)

- Predicting that it won't help (you need to examine the basis for this prediction and get agreement from the client(s) to test this out in action)

Note: Monitoring thoughts is a new skill for clients and at the start of the therapy they may find this difficult. Since this is not an activity people normally engage in, it is important that you help them to be patient and understand the value of practicing this skill in order to optimize this ability. One basic mindfulness skill utilizes increasing awareness of looking inward at thoughts in a non-judgmental way. This is an idea that can be easily integrated as part of CBT, and Chapter 5 will explore that concept.

Some clients may need considerable help from you in carrying this out. Any effort or small steps clients make in this regard should be reinforced. Many individuals already keep journals and this should be encouraged with the aim being to eventually get the client to clearly distinguish feelings from associated thoughts. If clients initially prefer to record thoughts in their own format, on an iPhone or in their own notebooks rather than on supplied CBT forms, this is acceptable, as the main purpose of helping them become more aware of their thoughts is still served. You should, however, always encourage them to record and clearly separate situations, feelings, and thoughts.

HELPING CLIENTS MODIFY THINKING

Identify the effects of thoughts

It is useful to look with the couple at the effects that certain thoughts or thinking processes can have in both the emotional and the behavioral arenas. This serves two purposes:

- It helps them recognize how dysfunctional thinking can have significant effects on mood and behavior.
- It provides a motivation to test and revise this thinking to a more healthy and functional set of cognitions.

The steps involved are as follows:

1. Identify a thought from a review of the **Identifying Thoughts and Feelings** worksheet, page 44.

   For example, the clients may identify the thought, "He doesn't want to change" or "She does these things deliberately to punish me."

2. Once the thought has been identified have the clients ask themselves the following questions:

   • What is the effect on me of having this thought?
   • What effect does it have on my emotions?
   • What effect does it have on my behavior?
   • What effect could this way of thinking have on our relationship?

   It may become obvious that these thoughts probably lead to irritation and frustration (emotional consequences) and may also result in behavioral consequences of not working as hard on the relationship or striking back, being defensive and acting in an irritated manner, which may in turn influence the other person's behavior (behavioral consequences).

3. Encourage both clients to look at the costs and benefits of having the thoughts and beliefs they have identified.

The worksheet, **Analyzing What Effects Thoughts and Beliefs Have on You**, on the next page is a helpful way to get the couple started on recognizing the effects, especially negative effects, of their thinking.

ANALYZING WHAT EFFECTS THOUGHTS AND BELIEFS HAVE ON YOU

Identified thought/belief: _____

_____

Degree of belief (0-100%): _____

_____

Advantages of holding this belief	**Disadvantages of holding this belief**
(How does it help me?)	(How does it hinder me?)
_____	_____
_____	_____
_____	_____
_____	_____
_____	_____
_____	_____
_____	_____
_____	_____
_____	_____
_____	_____
_____	_____
_____	_____
_____	_____
_____	_____
_____	_____

Copyright 2018 © John W. Ludgate & Tereza N. Grubr, *The CBT Couples Toolbox*. All Rights Reserved

For the moment, the **validity** of the thoughts is not being questioned, simply their **effects**. Generally, clients will be more motivated to do further work on challenging thoughts and beliefs when they see that there is a cost to carrying on with the same thinking and behavior patterns. For example, if this technique is used thinking, "I resent having to do so much in this relationship," while also wanting to stay in and enhance the current relationship may be seen by the client to be a discrepancy in need of resolution.

Note: In carrying out these interventions, make sure not to focus all of the attention on only one of the partner's maladaptive thinking. This will likely lead to one-upmanship and may be used against the partner whose issue is being focused on. It is important that you communicate that these interventions apply to each partner (and follow this practice in sessions). The observing partner's role is not to point out the distortions or inconsistencies in the other's beliefs in an adversarial way. Guided discovery by you and careful monitoring of the other partner's involvement, or working on two issues in tandem (one for each partner), will prevent this.

Modify the effects of thoughts

Having established that the thought is creating some costs (for example, creating frustration or preventing caring behaviors), you can now move on to modifying or countering the thoughts by means of several standard CBT methods. Identifying distortions in thinking can help clients distance themselves from their thinking and begin reappraising their thoughts.

The steps involved are:

- Have the clients become familiar with the concept of cognitive distortions by completing Learning About Cognitive Distortions (11 Ways to Make Yourself Miserable) on the next page. Sometimes, describing this phenomenon as "thinking styles" or "ways of thinking" avoids the perception that one is wrong, which the term "distortion" may imply. You might supply an example from your life to get across the idea that this is a common and frequent occurrence in people's thinking.

- Have each client identify any tendencies to engage in any particular distortions by writing down some personal examples as suggested in this handout.

- Examine an identified thought or set of thoughts collected from a recent upsetting situation which they have recorded on the **Identifying Thoughts and Feelings** worksheet on page 44 or which have come up in therapy.

- Label which distortion(s), if any, is evidenced in this thought or set of thoughts. For example, "He never helps me with anything," "She is late getting ready to punish or control me," are examples of over-generalizing, mind reading and personalizing, respectively.

- When the clients recognize the influence of the distortion, have clients respond to the initial dysfunctional thought(s) with a more adaptive thought. Example: "Since I know I may be personalizing her being late, I need to get more information about what she might have been doing while I was waiting to go."

In this way, the initial dysfunctional thought is replaced with an alternative response which is likely to be more helpful and functional.

The worksheet on page 52, **How to Recognize Distortions in Your Thinking**, can be used to record problem situations, feelings, thoughts and distortions as a means to facilitate cognitive reappraisal and re-framing.

Learning About Cognitive Distortions
(11 Ways to Make Yourself Miserable)

Cognitive distortions are inaccuracies in our thinking. We can think of our thoughts as representations of reality, sort of like a photograph. If we have a smudge on the lens of the camera, then the photo will show a picture that does not accurately represent what was in front of the camera. Even if the lens is clear but we take a picture of only part of an object, then the picture will not accurately portray the whole object.

It is safe to assume that everyone engages in cognitive distortions at times, especially during times of distress. It can be very helpful to be able to identify distortions in your thinking, because once you have discovered a distortion, you will know how to correct it and feel better. Identifying your cognitive distortions is like diagnosing a thought problem. A good diagnosis usually points to a helpful remedy. Below is a list of 11 common distortions with examples of how they might occur. See if you can identify one or more distorted thoughts of your own.

All or Nothing/Black or White: Seeing things as though there were only two possible categories.

Example: If a situation turns out imperfectly, you see it as a total failure. Your partner forgets to compliment you on an achievement and you think, "Well, he thinks nothing of anything I do."

Your example:

_____

_____

Over-Generalizing: A negative event is seen as part of a never-ending pattern of defeat.

Example: When your partner is late you think, "She never thinks of me and my feelings."

Your example:

_____

_____

Mental Filter: Seeing only negative aspects of a situation while screening out the positive aspects.

Example: You focus on a critical comment your partner made while ignoring all the positive feedback you received.

Your example:

_____

_____

Copyright 2018 © John W. Ludgate & Tereza N. Grubr, *The CBT Couples Toolbox*. All Rights Reserved

Jumping to Conclusions: Predicting things will go a certain way before you have the facts.

Example: Your partner looks at another man/woman in a restaurant and you assume he/she is looking for another partner and will leave you.

Your example:

_____

_____

_____

Mind-Reading: Assuming that you know exactly what someone is thinking.

Example: A friend or your partner seems irritated or not as pleasant as usual and you think, "He must be angry with me."

Your example:

_____

_____

_____

Fortune-Telling: Predicting that things will turn out badly and that you won't be able to cope.

Example: After an argument with your partner you imagine you both divorcing and you being alone and miserable.

Your example:

_____

_____

_____

Magnifying or Minimizing: Overvaluing or minimizing the importance of a situation or certain information.

Example: Even though you may be enjoying a nice time with your partner, you are upset by one or more things he/she said during the evening and you write off the whole evening.

Your example:

_____

_____

_____

Copyright 2018 © John W. Ludgate & Tereza N. Grubr, *The CBT Couples Toolbox.* All Rights Reserved

Emotional Reasoning: Assuming that how you feel is an accurate reflection of how things are.

Example: If you are feeling unloved at a particular time, you conclude that your partner does not love you or has stopped loving you.

Your example:

_____

_____

_____

Shoulds: You tell yourself things "should" or "shouldn't" be a certain way. We do this with ourselves, with other people, and with situations.

Example: "She/he should know what I want without me having to ask."

Your example:

_____

_____

_____

Labeling: This is an extreme form of all-or-nothing thinking which can be damaging to our self-esteem and our relationships.

Example: Instead of simply acknowledging a mistake, we say, "I'm such a screw-up" (substitute "loser," "idiot,"). Applying labels to ourselves or others ("that SOB") will tend to blind us to other qualities which we or others have.

Your example:

_____

_____

_____

Personalizing (Blaming): This distortion occurs when we hold ourselves entirely responsible for something that isn't or wasn't entirely under our control. When this process is reversed, we blame someone else entirely for a situation we have had a part in creating.

Example: "It's all my fault/all my partner's fault that we are not getting along."

Your example:

_____

_____

_____

Copyright 2018 © John W. Ludgate & Tereza N. Grubr, *The CBT Couples Toolbox.* All Rights Reserved

HOW TO RECOGNIZE DISTORTIONS IN YOUR THINKING

The next time you become upset or have a negative emotional reaction, see if you can identify both what you were thinking and any distortions in the thoughts on this worksheet.

Feelings

What was I feeling (angry, anxious, sad, etc)?

_____

_____

_____

_____

How bad was the feeling (0-100)?

_____

_____

_____

_____

Situation

Where was I? What was going on?

_____

_____

_____

_____

Copyright 2018 © John W. Ludgate & Tereza N. Grubr, *The CBT Couples Toolbox*. All Rights Reserved

Thoughts What went through my **mind**? What thoughts did I have?	Distortions Identify the distortion for each thought

Copyright 2018 © John W. Ludgate & Tereza N. Grubr, *The CBT Couples Toolbox*. All Rights Reserved

Testing the evidence

You can help your clients reality-test or check out the validity of their thoughts, when they involve assumptions or general conclusions.

- Identify the exact distortion or assumption the clients are making (for example, the assumption "She has no respect for me" or "He sees me as inadequate").

- Define the terms involved (in the example above, it may be important to know what "respect" and "inadequate" mean and how they would know if the opposite was shown). This step may reveal unrealistic expectations a client may have.

- Ask what the level of belief in the thought is on a scale of 0-100. Low-belief ratings can kick-start the process of seeing the other side (reasons why this thought is not valid or accurate). Also, this is a good baseline against which to later reassess the believability of these initial thoughts. Lastly, the more believable the thought, the more emotionally-arousing it is likely to be.

- List all the evidence which supports the assumption. In the above example, the data reviewed might include examples of behavior showing disrespect or statements which are seen to suggest inadequacy.

- List evidence which goes against the assumption. In these same examples, this might include times one partner has shown respect by defending the other partner ("She said yesterday that my boss had no right to treat me that way") or where an acknowledgement has been made of a specific competency ("He has said several times that I am good at money management or planning trips").

- Reconsider the original assumption and how much he/she now believes it. This cognitive intervention will often successfully challenge the over-generalized responding, which occurs when an event is taken out of context. The original thought can also be restated in a more accurate way: "She does respect me at times, but could show me more respect at these times and in these ways _____," "He probably doesn't see me as being incompetent all the time, but he could give me credit when it is deserved and be less critical when I can't do certain things like_____."

The next worksheet, **Reviewing the Evidence for Your Negative Thought(s)**, can be a very useful and systematic way of reviewing the evidence in session, and clients are also encouraged to complete it on their own when aware of strong negative thoughts underlying distress. It is strongly suggested that you use these forms and interventions with clients in session before assigning them for use at home to eventually complete on their own.

REVIEWING THE EVIDENCE
FOR YOUR NEGATIVE THOUGHT(S)

Write down the identified thought(s):

_____

_____

_____

_____

_____

Rate your degree of belief (0-100%): _____

List the evidence for and against your thought(s) in the boxes below:

Evidence Against	Evidence For

Now, rate your degree of belief in your original thought (0-100%): _____

Restate your original thought(s):

_____

_____

_____

_____

Copyright 2018 © John W. Ludgate & Tereza N. Grubr, *The CBT Couples Toolbox*. All Rights Reserved

Generating alternative viewpoints

This technique, also known as re-attribution, can be helpful in evaluating and modifying negative, rigid and emotionally-arousing explanations of events by considering other less negative interpretations.

Five steps to generate alternative viewpoints:

1. Identify exactly how clients are interpreting a stressful situation and what effect this interpretation is having. One example is a situation where one partner is late getting home and the other partner views this as an indication that the tardy partner doesn't care about their feelings or is doing something detrimental to the relationship. This interpretation can demoralize or anger the "offended" partner, who may then go on the offensive when the tardy partner does arrive before checking out other alternatives. Naturally, greater conflict ensues.

2. Encourage clients to brainstorm all other possible explanations for their partner's behavior. What else might explain their tardiness—could the traffic have been bad due to construction, or did the partner forget to charge their phone preventing a call home?

3. Help clients review the evidence to support each of these alternatives and estimate how likely it is that each contributed to the outcome.

4. Facilitate the process of coming up with a broader and less personal explanation for what happened based on the above. Restate the original thought in light of what now seems the most likely explanation.

5. Problem-solve what can be done to address these issues. In the above example, possible solutions may include always having a working cell phone or calling before leaving somewhere to give an estimation of likely arrival time if running behind.

The worksheet on the next page, **Generating Alternate Ways of Looking at Things**, will be helpful in facilitating the use of this cognitive technique.

GENERATING ALTERNATIVE
WAYS OF LOOKING AT THINGS

Write down the identified thought/interpretation:

_____

_____

_____

Rate your degree of belief (0-100%) _____:

List all other possible viewpoints or explanations. What is the evidence for each?

What are Other Explanations?	What is the Evidence?

Rate your degree of belief in the original thought now (0-100%): _____

Restated thought:

_____

_____

Is more information needed to decide which of the above is more likely or logical?

Yes _____ No _____

If so, how could this be obtained? Action plan:

_____

_____

Copyright 2018 © John W. Ludgate & Tereza N. Grubr, *The CBT Couples Toolbox*. All Rights Reserved

Decatastrophizing and de-awfulizing

If the thoughts identified in a client's analysis of a distressing situation involve some "what if" or "worst-case scenario" thinking, this technique can be very helpful in:

- More realistically assessing how likely this scenario actually is to happen.
- Considering how bad the consequences would be if it did actually happen.

The five steps involved are:

1. Identify with the client what future negative outcomes are being predicted. For example, after an argument with his/her partner a client might have the following automatic thoughts (linked with negative emotions): "This means he/she will turn against me, not speak to me for a long time, then our relationship will be ruined and we will end up divorced."

2. Have the client consider how likely it is that each of these will actually occur (decatastrophizing). In the above example, a client might make the following re-appraisal: "Based on past experience, he/she is likely to be mad with me and non-talkative for a while but leaving or divorcing is pretty unlikely."

3. Have the client also consider some of the worst outcomes and what the actual consequences would be (de-awfulizing). How awful would it actually be if that did happen?

4. What coping strategies could be used to deal with it? In the example above, the client might ask himself/herself, "Even if he/she did act this way, what then? How would I handle it? Would I be able to cope, recover or survive?"

5. Finally, have the client assess what the most likely outcome is (his/her best guess as to how things will go). In the example above, the client might conclude, "He/she will be unhappy for a while and then probably come around and be more communicative, and I can cope with the temporary stress."

This type of review clarifies for the client that the worst-case scenario may never come to pass but, if it does, that he or she may actually have resources for coping with it. This will lead to a reduction in emotional distress.

The **Decatastrophizing When Thinking the Worst** worksheet on the next page may be helpful for you to use in session and eventually for the clients to use on their own.

DECATASTROPHIZING
WHEN THINKING THE WORST

My worst fear	How likely is it (0-100%)?	What would I do if it happens?	What is the most likely outcome?

Copyright 2018 © John W. Ludgate & Tereza N. Grubr, *The CBT Couples Toolbox*. All Rights Reserved

CHAPTER 4:
Behavioral Interventions

Behavioral approaches have been utilized over many years in treating couples going back to Richard Stuart's work (Stuart, 1969) and represented in two seminal texts (Stuart, 1980; Jacobsen & Margolin, 1979). Also, a self-help book based on these principles (Christensen & Jacobsen, 2001) is highly recommended, as a very useful supplement to the approach outlined below.

While focusing on behavior, these strategies will produce far-reaching positive effects that directly change couples' attitudes, feelings, and beliefs. Among these are:

- Increase partner satisfaction
- Create positive emotions
- Show a willingness and commitment in each partner
- Change negative cognitions regarding the self ("I can't...."), the relationship ("It can't improve") and the partner ("He/she will never change")

Behavioral interventions include:

- Problem-solving
- Behavioral exchange
- Communication training
- Conflict resolution
- Anger control
- Assertiveness

Problem-solving

Jacobsen & Margolin (1970) developed a problem-solving procedure for couples outlining some strategies for successful conflict resolution. The principles described included setting an agenda, specifically defining problems, expressing problems in a positive way, discussing only one problem or solution at a time, focusing on solutions, not on blame, and seeking compromise. The general problem-solving approach (Nezu & D'Zurilla, 2012), as it is used in individual therapy, is also relevant here.

Communication training and problem-solving are often used in tandem. Learning to talk and listen effectively, which will be described later in the section on communication training, is a good first step towards using these skills to work together in problem-solving and probably should be done first.

Becoming more effective in solving problems can be an integral part of improving a couples' relationship and increasing relationship satisfaction. It can help to understand the problem-solving process and the stages of effective problem-solving. The following list summarizes the key elements.

The stages of effective problem-solving are:

- **Identification** of a problem (What specifically is the problem?)
- **Solvability** (Is it potentially solvable?)
- **Importance** (Is it an important issue or trivial?)
- **Goal** (What is the desired outcome?)
- **Possible solutions** (What are the options available?)
- **Pros and cons** (What is good and bad about each option?)
- **Selection** of the best option (Based on the pros and cons, what seems the best way forward?)
- **Implementation** of that option
- **Outcome** (How did it work?)
- **Return** to other solutions, as necessary

Following is an example of a completed **Effective Problem-Solving** worksheet done in session. As you see, the questions are designed to prompt problem-solving on behalf of the couple. This can be demonstrated in session first, taking a problem the couple faces. Then, have the couple use a blank worksheet (on page 65) for completion as a homework assignment.

- What is the specific problem you are trying to solve? *Not having any time together.*
- What is your goal? *Have at least two times a week when we spend an hour or longer together.*
- What are all the possible solutions or options?
    - *Date night (out)*
    - *Date night at home after the children go to bed*
    - *Saturday morning get up early before the kids do and talk over coffee*
    - *Have kids watch a movie early in the evening and hang out in the bedroom*
    - *Meet for lunch during the week*
- What is good and bad about each?
- Which are the best of these and how will we put it into action?
    - *Get up around 8:30 next Saturday, have breakfast without cell phones or TV on, and chat until the kids wake (usually 9:30)*
    - *Have lunch together next Wednesday at Tessa's Cafe*

Possible solution	Pros	Cons
Date night (out)	Nice to be away from home Go to a desired movie/restaurant	Time Cost Lack of privacy
Date night (home)	Inexpensive Convenient	Tired after kids in bed
Sat. morning	Good start to weekend As above, inexpensive, convenient	Like to sleep in Not at our best in a.m.
While kids watch movie	Easy to organize	Possible interruptions Some guilt re: not being with them for family time
Lunch during week	Away from home Paired with food we both like	Rushed due to work demands Lack of privacy

It is desirable that the couple ultimately will carry out this strategy without the therapist. To ensure good cooperation and also to maximize the chances that this becomes a well-practiced skill, it is important that there be lots of practice in session. Sometimes it can also be helpful to start with milder and less emotionally-driven issues (spending time together versus different views on child rearing). Problems addressed might also include creating romance and sexual intimacy, dealing with children, finances, independent activities or socializing.

In carrying this out, it is crucial that you do not supply solutions, but ask each partner questions like: "What are any ideas you have regarding this issue and how to resolve it?" Reinforcement should be provided for any suggestions, or a suggestion can be used as a springboard for asking a question to pursue similar ideas ("Apart from not having a vacation this year, which you suggested, is there any other luxury either of you think you could cut back on which might help the financial situation?") When it comes to the pros and cons or evaluation of possible solutions, you might first ask the person who came up with the idea to consider what's good and not so good about it before turning to the partner's view (this ensures better listening and less perceived criticism or one-upping).

At the stage when there are several possible solutions identified with pros and cons, ask each partner to select which one sounds best to them and, if there is consensus, select this as the option to try. This is also important when they do this on their own to maximize cooperation and prevent arguing.

There are a number of things for you to keep in mind during attempts at problem-solving:
  • Sometimes the problem is not equally shared and is more important to one or the other partner. It is important to compare perceptions of the problem, as there can be differing cognitions regarding importance and solvability.

- It is helpful to have both partners agree on a description of the problem.
- The problem needs to be defined in precise behavioral terms or in a non-negative way (versus the complaint).
- When brain-storming options, even far-fetched ideas are encouraged to help unstick the couple from the customary narrow range of solutions. You might want to ensure there are at least five or six options before moving on to evaluating them.
- When discussing the options, it may be that numbers one, two and three will appeal to partner A and three, four and five to partner B. Therefore, three is the most likely to work given some "buy-in" from both partners.
- It may be necessary to include the idea of a "trade off" if there are no mutually-agreeable solutions.

The outcome of problem-solving attempts can help assess how flexible the couple are and how well they can cooperate and prevent arguing or conflict.

Issues with problem-solving

Datillio & Padesky (1990) note that issues may come up when there is a power differential in the relationship. This procedure is based on a collaborative model of power equality, but this can be lacking in some relationships. This may come about because there is a belief that one, for example the male, should be in control. This will need to be explored. Style of influence in the relationship can be assessed and modified where necessary. The mutual problem solving procedure is likely to be more effective in terms of relationship satisfaction than the coercive methods they have used, where one partner tries to forcefully insist that this solution is the right one. Using a guided discovery approach, you can review with the couple the advantages of this approach which involves reciprocity versus these approaches the couple have used in the past. You may need to review with the couple the advantages and disadvantages of reciprocity versus the way the couple have been functioning by using a guided discovery approach. Additionally, power differences may come from cultural factors or family of origin learning experiences and these should be explored as well.

There are other common beliefs that can also sidetrack collaborative problem-solving, such as, "I have given in too much and won't any more," "This is unfair," or "The man/woman is supposed to decide."

Another dysfunctional assumption that can interfere with effective problem-solving is the idea that there is a perfect solution and, as a result, consideration should not be given to any others. Again, you can help the couple look at the costs and benefits of inaction versus engaging in a less than perfect action. Loosening the perfectionistic standards of one or both partners may be important.

Effective Problem-Solving

What is the specific problem we are trying to solve? _____

What is our goal? _____

What are all the possible solutions or options? _____

_____

_____

_____

_____

What is good and bad about each?

Possible solution	Pros	Cons

Which is the best of these and how will we put this into action?

_____

_____

_____

_____

Copyright 2018 © John W. Ludgate & Tereza N. Grubr, *The CBT Couples Toolbox*. All Rights Reserved

Behavioral exchange/reciprocity counseling

This method/procedure/idea model was first introduced by Stuart (1969) and is often used in behavioral approaches. This procedure is based on the principle of reciprocity and on the idea of increasing reinforcement in a mutual way. It is sometimes described as "giving to get."

Couples often experience a lack of reciprocity in their relationship and feel they do not get back what they put in. This leads to a "why should I, since he/she doesn't" mentality and there is often gridlock. By setting up an exchange the gridlock may be broken. The responsibility to be the initiator is taken away from the clients since you are setting it up and each individual has their part to play, independently of what the other is doing. If they do carry out the exchange, it can often have a dramatic effect on the couple's view of each other and their overall satisfaction. It can also lead to a spontaneous recall of other good things in their relationship now or in the past. It can set up positive expectation for change and it introduces collaboration where there may have been none. Notice that while this is a "behavioral" approach, it incorporates many of the ideas from other allied therapies, which is the beauty of an integrated approach.

Steps in setting up behavioral exchanges

- Identify the rationale for this approach and the need to change what is currently happening (the emphasis on the negative, critical comments, noticing undesirable behavior).
- Write out a list of small, positive behaviors each would like to ask of the partner. It is important that initially these are not behaviors tied into areas of conflict.
- Encourage each individual to specify exactly each behavior that they would like to receive from the partner. You can help facilitate this by asking: "What is one thing you would like your partner to do next week which would make you feel good/please you? Be specific in terms of what, when and where." It is important to make sure that the "doer" knows exactly what to do and the "receiver" will know when it happens.
- Encourage clients to come up with the positive version ("compliment me") rather than the negative version ("stop criticizing me").
- Get each to agree to do two to three things on the list for their partner.
- Have each initiate changes in their own behavior, irrespective of what the other does.
- Have each sign a contract for a series of specific exchanges (contingency contracts).
- Record the frequency of the desired behavior on a chart.
- Review what behaviors occurred, how it felt to the receiver and to the person engaging in the behavior, and what positive outcomes there were, if any.
- Assess how each stuck to the contract and what the effects were (how did the other person respond or experience the change).

You should stress that this is for self-improvement and relationship improvement rather than just to get something back. However, this may build up relationship credits rather than deficits which can be useful later. The couple is encouraged to view it as a behavioral experiment to see what happens when each does something nice for the other rather than just a way to change the other's behavior.

Examples of behavioral exchanges

- Give me a compliment once per day.
- Show affection physically (hug, kiss) when leaving or arriving.
- Spend 10 minutes with me without doing anything else once each day.

- Put the kids to bed every other night.
- Bring home or cook dinner twice a week.
- Attend church with me on Sunday.
- Plan a date once a week.

Related to this positive exchange is the idea of "catching your partner doing something nice" which involves each client noting and acknowledging anytime the partner acts in a positive way, whether the other partner asked for this or not. This can also lead to a positive exchange. Related to this is the idea of "caring days" (Stuart, 1980) where the couple agrees to act on certain days "as if" they cared as much for each other as at the best time in their relationship.

At this time, you can also ask each partner to indicate some behaviors they like that their partner is already doing (without being asked), even if these are low frequency in terms of occurrence.

An assigned homework might be:

- To become aware (regular mental check) of anything their partner did which is viewed as caring or desirable.
- Express how this felt ("I really liked it when you….").
- Put aside a short time period at the conclusion of each day when each will describe what they liked in the partner's behavior that day.

This practice can reverse the tendency of distressed couples to be primed to notice and selectively attend to negative or aversive behaviors in each other.

Possible problems with behavioral exchange

Some obstacles which may come up include the following:

- One or both clients takes the attitude "You first then me." Sometimes this can mean each partner stands on ceremony waiting for the other to start. Here you should go back to the rationale for this approach and revisit the costs-benefits of initiating positive behaviors independently of what the partner does.
- Some clients believe "It doesn't count when you have to ask; he or she should just know what I need." Here the therapist can speak about the difficulty and ineffectiveness of mind reading. The "pass the pepper" analogy is useful here. The couple is given the example of eating with someone when the pepper is closest to the other person and they would like to have the pepper to season their food. Rather than ask, they wait for the other person to notice that they need the pepper which may never happen.
- On occasion, clients will be skeptical about this technique, believing, "this is trivial and does not address our deeper problems." You may again go back to the rationale for this technique (the idea that creating even small positive exchanges can lead to other changes) and get across the notion that "the journey of a thousand miles starts with a single step."

Communication training

Communication training has played a pivotal role in behavioral approaches to relationship problems (Jacobsen & Margolin, 1979; Stuart, 1980) and fits easily with the CBT emphasis on skills training. Utilizing cognitive strategies, the therapist can look at beliefs as well as skill deficits which lead to communication problems. Skills training and cognitive interventions can be used together in a maximally effective manner, as will be described below.

Communication problems can have a major negative effect on relationship satisfaction. Poor communication is often what couples come for help with. It has been found to be the most frequent and damaging issue in relationship difficulties. Gottman (1994) found that couples considering divorce showed much more negativity than positivity in contrast to those who were in satisfying relationships.

Poor communication behaviors, following Gottman's research, includes:
- Complaints/criticism (being judgmental and blaming)
- Contempt (mocking, sarcasm, belittling)
- Defensiveness (self-protection from perceived attack by counterattack or denial)
- Stonewalling (being detached, cold, distant)

Burns (1988) outlines characteristics of bad communication. He cites 15 styles of communication which can be maladaptive. Among them are:
- Truth: Insisting that one is right and the other person is wrong
- Blame: A fixed assertion that the problem is the partner's fault
- Denial: Refusing to admit to being hurt or angry
- Defensiveness: Refusing to admit to any part in the problem
- Counterattack: Responding to a partner's criticism or comments by criticizing them back, sometimes on a different issue

Other "bad communication" behaviors are scapegoating, sarcasm, self-blame, demandingness, martyrdom and diversion. For a fuller description, the reader is encouraged to consult *Feeling Good Together* (Burns, 2010).

It is important to note that frequently a request for better communication from partners may translate to a belief that the other person or partner should concede or end up agreeing with him/her. It is important to help couples see that good communication does not necessarily involve or entail agreement, but is mutually beneficial in promoting better understanding, acceptance and more collaboration rather than constant disagreement and high conflict discussions where each wants their way or insists the other person sees that they are right.

You can establish a communication strategy through exercises practiced regularly in which each partner takes turns. Clients are coached in the qualities of being an effective speaker and listener. Feedback is sought about what it felt like to be communicated with in this different way. This can be more rewarding for each individual, as they may feel more respected and understood.

These principles can be given as a handout to the couple to read, practice and refer to. It is of vital importance that both the speaker and listener state his/her view briefly and in a calm tone, describing feelings/thoughts without blame or insults. This should involve "I" statements rather than "you" statements and a focus on the present issue rather than the past ("I don't like x or I feel y" rather than "You always….").

Again, both partners need to understand that good communication does not have to mean agreement. They can respectfully agree to differ but attempt to see where the other person is coming from.

Good communication, especially in situations of conflict, involves three vital steps, none of which should be skipped:

- Listen carefully with respect, empathy and an attitude of curiosity and openness
- Reflect on what was heard and summarize this to the partner
- Decide slowly and mindfully how to respond (agreement, apology, assertion)

Slowing down the rapid-fire communication which characterizes arguments and negative interactions is extremely important. In heated exchanges, partners are often not really listening, but assuming what is being directed at them and quickly responding to the **assumed message** rather than the **actual message**. A useful metaphor for couples is a tennis analogy. Before playing your shot, you have to wait to see where the previous shot from your opponent landed, not rush impulsively to the net or tram lines based on an assumption that this is how your opponent will play the ball. This would not be effective in playing tennis and likewise makes for ineffective and unhelpful communication.

Both of the following handouts can be given to couples to aid in practicing good communication skills as homework assignments.

PRINCIPLES OF EFFECTIVE COMMUNICATION

- Speak attentively, maintain eye contact, check for responses

- Be brief, get to the point, don't over-speak or dominate the conversation

- Ask meaningful questions to assist the exchange of ideas, not questions that have "yes" or "no" answers

- Accept silence

- Avoid cross-examination or finishing sentences for the other

- Be diplomatic and respectful

- Listen attentively and actively through the entire message from the speaker

- Give signals to indicate that active listening is taking place (maintaining eye contact, nodding head)

- Repeat back/summarize what has been heard ("You are feeling….")

- Look for the specifics of what was said rather than what it means or how it fits in with previous issues or your history ("This irritated you because…." rather than "This is your personality or background")

- Ask questions for clarification, if necessary ("Which was most upsetting to you?")

- Find points of agreement, if possible, or something that the listener can see as valid ("I can see how that would have been irritating")

- After some of the above occurs, slowly and carefully indicate a reaction to what is communicated or give an explanation of intentions, if appropriate ("I thought it might help you if I …. but I see that it didn't")

- Apologize, if necessary, or take some responsibility for what occurred ("I am sure that raising my voice was unhelpful and I am sorry that I did that") without a sting in the tail ("I am sorry for…. but you gave me no option")

- Even when not willing to take all the blame, express regret that your partner is hurt, sad or anxious

- When there is a continuing disagreement, the partners should ask themselves, "How important is it to confront this issue or my partner right now?" or "Which is most important, my ego/pride or our relationship?" (If perceived as not that important, you or your partner may decide to let it go.)

Copyright 2018 © John W. Ludgate & Tereza N. Grubr, *The CBT Couples Toolbox*. All Rights Reserved

TIPS FOR
EFFECTIVE COMMUNICATION

Desirable speaker behaviors

- Be brief

- Be specific

- State things as positively as possible

- Use "I" statements

- Make it clear what would be helpful

- Avoid global "You" statements

- No insults, blaming or accusations

- No labels or absolutes

- Check out inferences about partner's behavior or intentions

Desirable listener behaviors

- Listen attentively, don't interrupt until speaker is finished

- Give signals to indicate you are listening

- Try to get to the kernel of what partner is saying or feeling

- Summarize what you think was said

- Ask for extra information or corrections to your summary

- Don't be defensive or counterattack

- If appropriate, clarify reasons for behavior without excusing it

- Do not analyze partner's motives beyond wanting to express self

- Find points of agreement in addition to any disagreement

- Apologize if your behavior contributed to partner's upset or express regret that he/she is distressed

- Inquire what will help now

Copyright 2018 © John W. Ludgate & Tereza N. Grubr, *The CBT Couples Toolbox*. All Rights Reserved

As with any new skill, practice is required. For that reason you can have clients first rehearse and practice communication skills in session and then as homework assignments. You can set up role plays and practice involving hypothetical or reported conflict situations which are occurring in between sessions. Lots of opportunities to demonstrate and practice implementing these skills should be created. Clients may often acquire these skills incrementally, and they should understand that this will take time and effort.

Later, the clients can practice these skills in other interactions in their lives (work, social, family) to develop greater competency and familiarity with these new behaviors.

We recommend the following sequence of practice:

- Non-personal (partners take turns practicing active listening skills when the other is describing something such as a book they are enjoying or a good friend's vacation experience)
- Personal but non-conflictual (one has a problem at work)
- Personal when conflict or negative feelings are present (they disagree over how to discipline the kids or manage the finances)

In each case there is a review of what the speaker will do and what the listener will do based on the **Principles of Effective Communication** on page 70 before the couple engage in the homework.

The reason for starting with discussions of non-conflictual topics is to ensure that negative emotions don't sabotage the process or constructive skills. Clients with high levels of conflict may need to practice emotional regulation skills before they can move to personal conflict situations.

You should, as Dattilio (2010) points out, model good expressive and listening skills for the couple in your interactions with them. You might demonstrate both good and bad communication with the clients and ask them to reflect on the differences. This can promote more active learning (as will role plays), as opposed to more direct and didactic instruction.

Gottman & Gottman (1999) list some indicators that clients are communicating better and may not need further intervention:

- A reduction in criticism, contempt, defensiveness, stonewalling
- The ratio of positivity to negativity increases significantly
- The provision of a buffer so that anger is seen as a chance to get information, not an attack
- Utilizing "love maps" on a daily basis, where they learn about each other in a continuous manner
- The emergence of a "positive sentiment override" which means messages once seen as negative or triggering irritation can be viewed as neutral or positive (constructive feedback)
- Partners "turning towards" rather than "turning away" and maintaining an emotional connection, even when they are not in agreement
- The use of a soft, not a harsh, tone when dealing with conflict
- Learning how to soothe the partner and the self

You should monitor whether these outcomes are being achieved and give feedback to the couple regarding progress. The important measure of progress is whether these are occurring outside the sessions without your direct intervention to promote these behaviors.

Some common difficulties experienced with communication training

One issue which can arise in this phase of couples therapy is that clients sometimes have difficulty being able to experience or convey empathy towards their partner, which is a pre-requisite for intimacy and positive exchange and leads to validation (Datillio, 1990). These clients may need a lot of practice in trying to see things from their partner's point of view. You can facilitate this by using role reversal exercises in which the client plays the partner and you or the other partner plays the client. Then you can ask what it feels like when the client is on the receiving end of, for example, a lot of personal criticism.

Another related issue is lack of validation, specifically a client not verbally acknowledging how the partner feels. Validation of a partner (Fruzetti, 2006) is not an agreement or apology. It is a communication that acknowledges the other person's view or feelings without necessarily agreeing.

Interruptions from clients during their partner's attempts to communicate in or outside sessions can be a problem. This is especially likely when emotion is high. If this occurs in session, you need to coach or prompt appropriate behavior. In some cases, using cues such as hand signals to remind him/her that the other person now "has the floor" may be necessary. The use of a paper and pencil (or pen) as described by Datillio (2010) may help to engage the listening partner who wants to interrupt. The listener writes down what they are feeling or thinking, and what they want to say and refrains from interrupting right then.

Another problem to be addressed may involve intense affect in session which interferes with effective communication. Deficits in emotional regulation can be countered by teaching some DBT skills to reduce high affect (anger, anxiety, frustration) before communication or active listening is attempted. This will be described in Chapter 5. On occasion, you may need to use a pre-arranged "time out" when emotions are intense. At this point, the couple will be instructed not to interact but to individually work on emotion regulation by using relaxation, mindfulness, self-soothing or recording thoughts and feelings under your direction. Beck (1988) describes "color mapping" where: **blue** represents being calm and easy to communicate with, **yellow** indicates some control but having more difficulty communicating with, and **red** signals a loss of control of emotions with a tendency to attack verbally or physically and with many cognitive distortions in operation. Inter-session practice in emotional regulation should begin in the "blue zone" rather than in the "yellow zone." You need to rehearse with the clients those strategies which can be used to transition from the red to the yellow zone. You can implement these in session when intense emotion occurs, in order to model what they can do on their own.

There can be many cognitions or automatic thoughts which can interfere with good communication. Interfering beliefs may fall into the following categories:
- **Hopelessness:** (The relationship, partner or individual can't change or, "the problems are too deep or too ingrained.") You need to work on the hopelessness and pessimism cognitively by testing out these assumptions and reviewing the evidence.
- **Inability to tolerate emotional discomfort in self or other:** ("Any distress has to be avoided at all costs" or "I am bad/my partner is bad if unpleasant feelings are created.") Again, cognitive techniques can be used to test this out or an exposure exercise can be introduced to show that it is not catastrophic to experience discomfort and may lead to a positive outcome.
- **Fear of intimacy or closeness:** ("I will be vulnerable if I share feelings," "I will be rejected," or "It is better to stay distant as it is too risky to talk about emotions.") This can also be subject to testing out and cognitive re-appraisal.

Conflict resolution skills

A number of effective communication skills and problem-solving strategies can be utilized in conflict resolution. Clients need to be trained in:

- Noticing early warning signals of escalation (their own feelings/behaviors and their partner's)
- Recalling the listening and expressive skills that can be used to de-escalate conflict (for example: no scapegoating, requests not complaints, asking clarifying questions)
- Practicing in advance phrases or behaviors that can end conflict gracefully (Fruzetti, 2006) such as saying, "We are better than this and should stop now in the interests of our relationship which is important to us."
- Engaging in adaptive, strategic withdrawal but with a rationale given to the partner ("I am feeling a bit out of control right now; I will go outside for a while and I will be ready to talk about this more calmly later.")

When upset or overwhelmed, people have difficulty recalling soothing or useful conflict-resolving language and tend to go into a threat-based habitual pattern of blaming, sarcasm, counterattack and defensiveness. This is a way to protect themselves but, if what needs to be protected is the relationship and their mutual caring, then some rehearsed phrases that allow one or both to extricate themselves from the destructive cycles may be very helpful.

Suggested phrases are:

"We are really hurting each other here, and I don't want that to continue."

"We care too much for each other to continue this. Can we stop?"

"I am feeling so sad now and I know you are upset. Can we find a way out?"

"I love you and don't want to go down this path."

These all are graceful ways to try to end conflict (Fruzetti, 2006) and involve an ability to see the bigger picture and accept the other person even with the ongoing conflict and behaviors that are unpleasant.

Possible problems in conflict resolution

- *The fallacy of the "last word."* This is common in distressed couples who believe they need to have the last word or need to say "one final thing" which escalates conflict further.
- *Being right rather than being effective.* As mentioned previously, many couples hold onto the idea that someone is right and someone is wrong even at the expense of their relationship.
- *The insistence that "everything has to be resolved right now."* This idea will prevent couples from adapting a strategic "time out" to work on reducing their affect before returning more calmly later to work on the conflictual issues.

It can be helpful to discuss all of the above in sessions to find more adaptive and effective ways to function in a relationship. Sometimes it is even helpful to have clients practice saying, "I don't know how to respond, give me a minute to consider what you said," to slow the process down and prevent the rapid-fire reactivity that creates conflict escalation.

In addition, judgments and meanings about conflict can cause secondary problems ("She/he can't love me if she/he acts this way." "There should not be conflict in a good relationship." "I must fix this immediately and be the peace keeper.") and these dysfunctional thinking patterns need to be addressed cognitively. This again illustrates the interweaving of the behavioral and cognitive procedures.

Anger control

Anger and dysregulated emotions can be major obstacles in achieving positive outcomes when using some of the techniques outlined in this workbook, which would otherwise be expected to help clients. Clients often have issues with anger in themselves and/or in their partner.

The following handouts can be given to clients dealing with anger issues. You and the couple can discuss key points after they have been read.

GUIDELINES FOR DEALING WITH ANGER IN YOURSELF

- Recognize early warning signals of anger, the "yellow zone" (usually characteristic bodily feelings) before it gets to the "red zone," when it is intense.

- Use coping strategies to deal with these early warning signals such as breathing, relaxation, mindfulness or taking a brief "time out" where you get involved in a distracting or soothing activity away from the anger-eliciting situation.

- Think about any other sources of your anger beyond the current provocation (the fact you can't go golfing because of the weather or kids acting up earlier) in addition to what someone is saying to you right now.

- When you have identified the situation triggering the anger ask yourself:
  - What does it mean to you that this occurred?
  - What were your expectations in this situation?
  - Were these realistic?
  - What do you feel you are entitled to in this situation?
  - Is this realistic?
  - If you have the idea something was unfair, was it unfair from the other person's perspective?
  - Was there any intention to treat you badly?
  - Are you responding to some other person or situation from your past?
  - How important is this in the big picture?

- What do you hope to achieve with your anger? What are the costs and benefits of feeling or acting angrily? Can you achieve what you need in another way?

- If your feelings of anger are justified:
  - Give yourself permission to feel angry/accept the feeling while coming up with a plan to deal with it.
  - Assert yourself in a controlled way.
  - Avoid being passive (and subsequently annoyed with yourself) or explosive (with negative consequences for the relationship).
  - State how you feel in a controlled tone using "I" statements and what you would like to happen (requests not demands).
  - Ensure your body language supports your assertive message.

- Take responsibility for feelings of anger, accept them and find a solution which should not involve insisting that the other person changes/apologizes.

Copyright 2018 © John W. Ludgate & Tereza N. Grubr, *The CBT Couples Toolbox*. All Rights Reserved

DEALING WITH ANGER IN
A PARTNER/OTHER PERSON

- Recognize early signs of anger in the other person.

- Inquire about these feelings in a non-critical way once you have observed them.

- Allow some ventilation; don't interrupt, become defensive, or try to problem-solve immediately.

- Display listening signals and reflect back how the other person appears to be feeling. Ask for clarification or confirmation.

- Don't invalidate the other person's feelings.

- Realize that anger is often displaced or cumulative. Ask if there are other sources of frustration without denying the present message.

- Disarm the anger by finding any points of agreement and, if appropriate, acknowledge your role in the anger episode.

- If the emotional level is too high for a problem-solving discussion, suggest a deferment with an agreed time to follow up.

- Check out what expectations the angry individual had for you (or others) and how they wanted to be treated.

- If the complaints are justified even in part, apologize for your part. Express regret that this occurred rather than taking 100% responsibility.

- State your own position non-defensively and calmly. Clarify your motives but don't punish or counterattack. Listen carefully, be supportive, but assert yourself respectfully and in a controlled way.

Copyright 2018 © John W. Ludgate & Tereza N. Grubr, *The CBT Couples Toolbox*. All Rights Reserved

ASSERTIVENESS

What does it mean to be assertive? It's important to help clients understand that positive self-expression and standing up for one's boundaries are vital communication skills. Many clients don't understand the full meaning of what assertiveness means in the context of their relationship. For example, clients may be intimidated, avoid speaking up and remain passive in their relationships. They may be habitually unassertive, fearful of the consequences of assertiveness, or feel it is "aggressive" to assert oneself. Many clients move from passive to explosive/angry if they have no "third gear" (assertion). They are avoidant of conflict or expressing any feelings for a period, but eventually are triggered into behavioral excesses such as shouting, yelling and being explosive and out of control. It is important to demonstrate both the key differences between, and the cost and benefits of, passivity, assertion and aggression. There are often negative consequences of resentment building up as it turns to passive-aggressive behavior. Passive-aggression is an indirect and unhealthy form of communication; aggression and attack is a direct but unhelpful form of communication; assertion is both direct and controlled (as well as respecting the other person) and thus more likely to be helpful.

When clients are characteristically unassertive, it may point to low self-esteem or general avoidance, which are issues that can be dealt with using CBT.

If therapy includes some assertiveness training, the following should be kept in mind:
- Assertiveness training should crucially involve positive expressiveness and not just negative assertion (being able to show appreciation and gratitude to a partner rather than just pointing out some unacceptable or unpleasant behavior).
- The emphasis should be on changing oneself by being assertive rather than trying to control the other person. It is a bonus and a secondary positive consequence if the other person changes.

Specific guidelines on how to be assertive are described in many sources (Alberti & Emmons, 1994), but include:
- Using "I" statements not "you" statements
- Being specific about the reason for assertion
- Turning complaints into requests
- Supporting the verbal message with congruent non-verbal signals (posture, eye contact, tone of voice)

Role plays and structured exercises can be a useful way to build up assertiveness skills, sometimes beginning with non-partner related situations (bad service in a restaurant, a friend not paying back money).

When clients are encouraged to be more assertive with each other, in session and outside therapy, it is important to ensure that there is no recrimination for greater self-expression. Clients, when they notice feelings coming on which they would characteristically avoid or suppress, can be coached in expressing these in a controlled way. The outcome may often allay their catastrophic fears about "opening up."

CHAPTER 5:
DBT, Mindfulness and Related Interventions

In this chapter we will discuss some applications of what are sometimes referred to as "third wave" therapies (DBT, ACT, Mindfulness) with couples. Let's take a brief survey of these, and examine how they fit as complementary approaches to CBT and behavioral therapies.

Dialectical Behavior Therapy (DBT) was first described by Marsha Linehan in the seminal book *Cognitive Behavioral Therapy for Borderline Personality Disorder* (1993). Having trained as a behavior therapist, she found more traditional cognitive and behavior therapies with their explicit focus on change were not as successful with Borderline Personality Disorder (BPD). The defining characteristics of DBT are: (1) a therapeutic emphasis on dialectics which involves the reconciliation of opposites in a continuous synthesis (for example, a client finding a balance between their expectations and their own capabilities), (2) an emphasis on acceptance and tolerating distress as a balance to change, and (3) a focus on validation, where an attempt is made to understand the client's world and acknowledge their feelings, thoughts and behaviors and how they make sense, given their life history and situations. DBT is strongly based on concepts from mindfulness and acceptance that involve a non-judgmental, observing approach. Lastly, clients are encouraged to develop improved behavioral repertoires and develop skills in the following areas:

- Emotion regulation
- Distress tolerance
- Interpersonal effectiveness
- Mindfulness

As you can see, this therapy incorporates CBT and behavioral methods. DBT has a strong evidence base and research shows it to be effective with BPD and other conditions. DBT has been applied to the treatment of adolescents (Miller, 2004) and anxiety/depression (Marra, 2004). Importantly, it has also been applied to the treatment of marital problems (Fruzetti, 2006).

Acceptance and Commitment Therapy (ACT) was developed by Steven Hayes and colleagues (Hayes, Strosahl & Wilson, 1999). While this therapy is based on Relational Frame Theory (an empirically-substantiated account of human behavior, language and cognition), ACT does not explicitly target modification of the client's feelings, thoughts and physiological reactions. Rather than change the reactions themselves it attempts to alter the function of these internal reactions by encouraging clients to view these as internal experiences, which are distinct from the self. It also promotes the idea that change in such feelings or thoughts is not necessary in order to make behavioral choices in line with one's goals and values. The acronym ACT refers to Accept, Choose and Take Action, which are the main components of this approach, which also incorporates a mindfulness orientation.

How does ACT differ from more traditional CBT? Here are a few key distinctions worth noting:

- ACT places a greater focus on awareness of experience of feelings and thoughts.
- ACT emphasizes mindfulness and acceptance instead of change.

- ACT fosters the development of an accepting, observational stance to feelings and thoughts instead of controlling or judging.

- ACT attempts to reduce experiental avoidance (avoiding feelings and thoughts).

- ACT encourages values-based living with emotions rather than managing or controlling emotions and avoiding life.

What CBT and ACT (and DBT as well) have in common is that they teach how to be less reactive to emotions and to observe one's thinking. They look at how behaviors and actions are helpful or harmful. Both DBT and ACT stress the importance of acceptance and mindfulness. ACT has a strong evidence base and has been used effectively for many conditions including depression, specific anxiety disorders and pain. It has also been applied to couples (Walser & Westrup, 2009; Gehardt, 2012).

Mindfulness, as a therapy intervention, was first described by Kabat-Zinn (1990), and served as an integral part of his Mindfulness-Based Stress Reduction (MBSR) approach. It now has a well-established research base and has become part of the therapeutic treatment for many psychiatric disorders.

Mindfulness has been described by Kabat-Zinn as "Paying attention in a particular way, on purpose, in the present moment and non-judgmentally." Individuals and couples can benefit from mindfulness practice. Carson et al (2004) and Barnes et al (2007) demonstrate a correlation between mindfulness practice and enhanced relationships in couples, including greater acceptance of each other, increased closeness, greater autonomy and more generally increased relationship satisfaction.

In couples therapy, the treatment plan can include the use of mindfulness to help each individual and additionally the relationship. Both individuals should be introduced to the principles of mindfulness early in therapy, which should then become a routine practice for both individually and in their interactions.

INTRODUCING MINDFULNESS TO CLIENTS

You should outline the purpose of mindfulness meditation and correct any misconceptions about what it is. The potential benefit and the need for practice should be stressed.

The next two handouts, **Mindful Breathing and Sitting Meditation**, are tools to help introduce your clients to mindfulness practices.

- Mindful Breathing may be done initially in session and practiced as homework.

- The Sitting Meditation script can be used with your clients during the session and then can continue as a homework practice assignment.

MINDFUL BREATHING

Mindful breathing is a great start to mindfulness in general and can be done in quite a short time. It can be very enjoyable and beneficial. It is important to understand that you are not trying to perfect this; just to benefit from it in regards to feeling some calm renewal.

Find a relaxing position. The back should be straight, not bent, with the back of the neck aligned to the spine and feet resting flat on the floor. Focus your attention on breathing, noticing each breath as it is taken in and let out.

When your attention settles on the breath, letting it be itself and not forcing it to go any particular way, breathing calms, and the mind reaches a place of more tranquility and peace. Mindful breathing sends the brain a message that everything is OK and there is no need to worry or fret.

"First, let your awareness drop down to your abdomen, away from all thinking and the cares of your day. Simply let your body breathe in and out exactly as it wants to. Just notice the flow of air in as you inhale and out as you exhale. Notice the rise and fall of your abdomen as you breathe. Notice the inflection point just before you begin to exhale and the pause before your body begins another cycle. Focus on what is interesting or pleasant about these sensations and concentrate as best you can on only that. When your mind pulls you away on to some other thoughts or focus of attention, notice this happening and gently come back to the breath without any recrimination for the wandering of your mind.

The goal of this exercise is not to obtain perfect concentration on the breathing. Rather it is to notice in a kindly way when your mind is wandering and return gently to the breath. By not struggling against the mind's natural tendency to wander, but simply observing it, we can develop heightened awareness which in itself is good practice.

Cultivate the sense that, with each breath, you are nourishing the cells in your body and building a calm mind and spirit. Continue as long as is comfortable for you, mindfully breathing in and out, noticing what it feels like, bringing your mind gently back to the breath when it wanders and enjoying what is happening right now without thought or judgment."

Copyright 2018 © John W. Ludgate & Tereza N. Grubr, *The CBT Couples Toolbox*. All Rights Reserved

SITTING MEDITATION

"In this exercise, choose a quiet place. Sit in a way that allows you to be both alert and relaxed. Allow a little time for transitioning from what you had been doing to the meditative state. Have an unhurried attitude towards this. Take a moment to become aware of the environment around you ... the sights, sounds, whatever is present there. Note the sensations in your body as you sit there. Feel the air on your skin. Notice any sensations emanating from how you are sitting or where your feet touch the floor or your back touches the chair.

Gently allow your awareness to settle in your abdomen or alternatively the point where air enters your nostrils. Notice as before the body breathing in and breathing out, letting the breath unfold of its own accord. Attend clearly to the pleasantness of this. If you notice, as you may, that your mind has wandered from your breath, briefly notice what you were thinking about or just say to yourself "thinking, thinking." Similarly, if you feel something, perhaps a physical feeling or an emotion such as anxiety, just notice it or say to yourself "feeling, feeling." Then gently return your attention to your breathing. The most important thing to realize is that such wandering is completely natural and to be expected. So do not engage in accusations against yourself for this. The aim is mere recognition or observation, not evaluation or judgment. The essence of this practice is to simply notice and return, notice and return as many times as is required without involvement in the content of what you are thinking or feeling.

Repeat this process for a comfortable period of time. Proceed slowly and only continue as long as is comfortable for you. As time goes on, your capacity to sit with yourself will gradually increase. Whatever you can manage, do it for that period of time every day if possible, gradually lengthening your meditation periods to at least 30-40 minutes. You may want to use a recording or written instructions to get you started and then follow the format described here on your own when you are ready. This allows you to complete a mindfulness practice anywhere anytime.

When you finish your meditation, take your time coming out and see if you can bring the same attitude of clear accepting awareness into your daily life. During the day and evening, return to your meditation by practicing a few mindful breaths. Opportunities may present themselves during the day to practice, such as when waiting in a bank or store, waiting for someone to pick up the phone, waiting in your car for traffic to start moving. These are good opportunities to practice with obvious benefits to you."

Copyright 2018 © John W. Ludgate & Tereza N. Grubr, *The CBT Couples Toolbox*. All Rights Reserved

MINDFULNESS FOR COUPLE INTERACTIONS

After the couple has practiced mindfulness exercises, you can teach them how to use these skills to enhance and improve their relationship.

As described by Fruzetti (2006), this phase of therapy will involve getting both partners to learn and practice the following skills:

- **Pay attention fully** to the partner and don't be distracted by one's own reactions
- **Observe,** don't judge
- **Notice and describe,** don't evaluate, appraise or label ("noticing and describing" leads to **curiosity and willingness to understand more** while "judging" leads to premature closure and negative feelings)
- Focus on **actions and data** (what was actually said or done) rather than interpretations or judgments
- Use mindfulness in positive or neutral situations before proceeding to negative or conflictual interactions

VALIDATION AND INVALIDATION

The concepts of validation and invalidation are a keystone of DBT practice, where clients are shown how to validate their own feelings and replace shame and judgment regarding feelings with acceptance. Self-validation has been found to be an effective and useful skill across a variety of situations. In the context of interpersonal issues, self-validation and other-validation are very important (Fruzetti, 2006). It has been found that self-validation often creates the conditions for more validation and acceptance of the partner. In contrast, invalidation of one's own feelings or one's partner's feelings can make a bad situation worse.

Consider the following example:

> *Rob was really looking forward to spending some intimate time (a shared activity such as watching a favorite show, cuddling on the sofa with a glass of wine and maybe making love later) with his partner, Jenny. He waited for her to finish reading their daughter a bedtime story and eventually realized that she had fallen asleep, along with their daughter, on the bed. He started to feel upset and later, when she woke up and joined him in bed, he was not comforted by her apology. Instead he barely spoke and gave her the "silent treatment." She in turn became angered by his response and a full-scale argument broke out.*

> *In this sequence, Rob did not self-validate his own initial distress. He did not allow himself to feel disappointed or soothe himself while distressed. Instead he suppressed the feeling by thinking "big deal, she is not interested anyway" but this, in turn, led to anger and caused him to silently seethe in the other room. When Jenny said that she was sorry that they had missed out on their time together, he also did not accept and validate her feelings of disappointment or regret and continued to invalidate both his own feelings and hers. She then, in turn, responded to him in a non-accepting and invalidating way that caused the argument to continue. Jenny could have recognized his disappointment, processed it, and acknowledged this in a gentle, validating way. She could also have accepted and acknowledged how they both felt, what feelings they shared (disappointment) and validated this. Rob or Jenny engaging in these validating behaviors would likely have brought them closer rather than creating a separation.*

Steps in self-validation

Both partners are encouraged to work on:

1. Developing better awareness of feelings, noting early signs of emotional arousal or an urge to attack.

2. Validating these feelings without judgment and showing compassion to themselves.

3. Accepting needs and wants in the moment as valid.

4. Coming up with strategies that will help them through these feelings.

Steps in partner validation

Next, each partner is instructed to work on:

1. Noting and describing to themselves the partner's actions and feelings as they are, rather than as they would like them to be. This encourages accepting the reality of the situation instead of what was hoped for or expected. (Note how this manages expectations just as CBT helps one become aware of "should" thinking distortions.)

2. Asking themselves what the partner might be experiencing now and recognizing how they may be hurting or feeling distressed.

3. Riding out the urges to counterattack, which also includes validating to themselves how hard it is to not react negatively, but to do the opposite.

4. Instead of suggesting or declaring what the partner should feel or what they need to do, disclosing their own feelings of hurt and asking about the partner's feelings in a non-judgmental way.

5. Reminding themselves of what they would like to have happen overall in the big picture (to be closer to this person) or what their longer-term relationship goals are and then speaking to this rather than to the immediate hurt (which will pass).

You can give your clients the following exercises to work on self-validation, partner validation or to repair validation when it has been broken.

SELF-VALIDATION EXERCISE

The next time you are upset, ask yourself:

What happened? _____

What exactly am I feeling (not why or what it means)? _____
_____

Then consider that is perfectly OK to feel as you do. Consider how you can get yourself through this feeling.

List actions (self-soothing and other) that might help: _____

_____

_____

_____

_____

_____

_____

_____

_____

_____

_____

_____

_____

_____

_____

_____

_____

_____

Copyright 2018 © John W. Ludgate & Tereza N. Grubr, *The CBT Couples Toolbox*. All Rights Reserved

PARTNER VALIDATION EXERCISE

When you are upset with your partner or the relationship, ask yourself:_____

What happened? _____

What feelings do I have? _____

_____

How can I accept these and understand them? _____

_____

How can I show compassion to myself (what might I say to an upset friend)? What can I do to self-validate or self-soothe? _____

_____

What is my partner feeling now? Why is this so upsetting for him/her?_____

_____

What do I notice in his/her actions/expressions? _____

_____

What can I say to myself that is compassionate, not judgmental, about what he/she is feeling?

_____

_____

What is the big picture? What is my overall feeling towards this person versus what I feel right now? What are my hopes for our relationship?

_____

_____

How can I create and show acceptance to him/her even if the actions are upsetting?

_____

_____

What actions can I engage in that will show acceptance? _____

_____

_____

Copyright 2018 © John W. Ludgate & Tereza N. Grubr, *The CBT Couples Toolbox*. All Rights Reserved

EXERCISES FOR REPAIR
IF INVALIDATION OCCURRED

What invalidating actions did I engage in (rather than what the other person did)?

_____

_____

What would have been more validating?

_____

_____

While forgiving myself for my actions then, what actions could I take now that would help repair our connection or relationship?

_____

_____

What can I tell my partner that is more validating now?

_____

_____

Copyright 2018 © John W. Ludgate & Tereza N. Grubr, *The CBT Couples Toolbox*. All Rights Reserved

One important aspect of mindfulness practice, that of describing rather than judging or evaluating, dovetails easily with the interventions used in CBT where thoughts are challenged and viewed as assumptions rather than facts. For example, in couples communication clients may "read into" their partner's comments. For instance, one partner says, "I would like it if you let me know you are going to be late coming home in the evening," but this is interpreted by the other as, "She wants to control me." Time can be spent in conjunction with the mindfulness practice on the issue of not judging or jumping to conclusions about one's partner's behavior. This fosters good communication.

You might introduce the difference between assumptions and facts by giving the following examples.

When individuals are reading, they often speed read and do not actually read every word. They assume that a sentence which starts with "Gazing into her eyes, he moved towards her and slowly...." is likely to end with, "kissed her." In a similar way, couples who have been with each other for some time often finish each other's sentences (in their mind, if not verbally). This usually works out OK, but may sometimes involve making a false prediction. When this takes the form of quickly judging each other's actions it can lead to pre-emptive emotions and behavior that is unhelpful. Consider the following interpersonal communication: The husband comes home late from work three nights in a row. His wife starts to say, "You work such long hours at your job and _____." Because he is feeling badly about being home late and already tense and on the defensive, he thinks she is going to end the sentence with, "I am sick of it." He assumes this outcome and may be feeling irritated by this and so cuts her off saying, "I don't want to hear it." However, what she had actually intended to say was "You work such long hours at your job, and I was thinking we should get away for the weekend."

Using mindfulness tools to facilitate clients being in the moment listening for what is actually said and noting the non-verbal information, such as facial expression and tone of voice, might prevent such jumping to conclusions and make for better communication patterns.

EMOTION REGULATION

Emotion regulation is an important part of DBT, and increasingly a part of CBT practice. In couples work, training both partners in these skills is likely to be very helpful for dealing with conflictual situations that elicit strong emotions.

It is often helpful to first discuss the role of emotions with clients. Here are some key points to share with clients when exploring emotions:

- Emotions can have positive effects in that they alert us to the need for action or protection.
- Emotions are not the enemy, but they can become problematic if they lead to negative consequences, such as aggression, avoidance or substance abuse.
- It is important to be aware of both initial emotions and secondary emotions, which are emotions about emotions.
- Invalidating or judging your own (or your partner's) emotions harshly is unhelpful.
- Through practice, you can learn to recognize at-risk situations for certain emotions (recognizing that any criticism can lead to irritation) or individual vulnerabilities to particular emotions.

- Mindfulness of emotions is a skill that is well worth practicing and this involves changing judgments about emotions to acceptance.
- Validation strategies, as described earlier, can be a major part of helping to manage emotional distress.

The next worksheet, **Dealing with Emotional Distress**, can be a useful exercise to help clients identify and analyze moments of high emotion. The handout **Guidelines for Managing Negative Emotions** on page 92 can be given to clients to illustrate the principles of effective emotion regulation.

DEALING WITH EMOTIONAL DISTRESS EXERCISE

Go through the following exercise when you experience high emotion.

Notice as early as you can the warning signs of beginning to get upset, then ask yourself:

What thoughts am I having that are leading to my distress?

_____

_____

Are these valid or accurate? _____

If I am predicting something, how likely is it to actually turn out that way? _____

Are these thoughts helpful to me and the relationship? _____

What can I say to myself that involves acceptance and mindfulness of the emotion?

_____

_____

_____

_____

_____

What activities could I involve myself in now that might help?

_____

_____

_____

_____

Copyright 2018 © John W. Ludgate & Tereza N. Grubr, *The CBT Couples Toolbox*. All Rights Reserved

What things would be soothing to me given how I feel? Anything physically self-soothing (relaxation, yoga, breathing)? List below:

_____

_____

_____

_____

_____

Anything mentally self-soothing (distraction, visualization, compassionate self-talk, phrases I could say to myself, things to remind myself of)? List below:

_____

_____

_____

_____

_____

Anything soothing involving the senses (scented candles, music, warm bath, taste of something I like)? List below:

_____

_____

_____

_____

Copyright 2018 © John W. Ludgate & Tereza N. Grubr, *The CBT Couples Toolbox*. All Rights Reserved

GUIDELINES FOR MANAGING NEGATIVE EMOTIONS

- Recognize what is being experienced.

- Give yourself permission to feel this.

- Examine underlying thoughts.

- Plan and engage in:

  - Activities that refocus attention away from feelings and are likely to produce some sense of accomplishment.

  - Activities that are pleasurable and may lead to mood improvement.

- Accept the feelings while being aware of the impermanence of this level of distress and determine to carry on with activities despite the feelings.

- Don't add to negative feelings with secondary emotional reactions (frustration or anxiety because of the initial feeling).

- Watch out for exacerbating thoughts such as "It's not fair," "Why me?" "It will never change," "It's my fault," or "It's his/her fault."

- Develop self-soothing strategies:

  - Peaceful imagery

  - Relaxation/meditation

  - Pleasurable, distracting activities

  - Sensory experiences

  - Distracting thoughts

  - Connecting with/contributing to others

Copyright 2018 © John W. Ludgate & Tereza N. Grubr, *The CBT Couples Toolbox*. All Rights Reserved

In a more general way, mindfulness and acceptance techniques facilitate (a) awareness of experience (somatic, affective, cognitive), (b) helping clients just notice experiences, or categorize them but not judge them, and (c) recognizing their impermanence (seeing feelings as clouds moving across the sky).

Mindful acceptance has been found to encourage distancing or defusion from internal events, creating a healthy distancing or de-centering from thoughts and feeling. It fosters a non-judgmental acceptance of subjective experience, since it often attempts to control or stop thoughts and feelings may be counterproductive.

Mindfulness can also be a form of exposure where clients are instructed to "stay with" feelings without judgment or an attempt to control them. They may also be encouraged to engage in "opposite action" (behavior that is the opposite from the normal action tendencies associated with one's emotions). This has obvious implications in couples work where, for example, when angry, a partner may be encouraged to speak in a soft, compassionate tone to the partner rather than the loud, insistent tone they would have normally used when angry.

Lastly, mindfulness can foster clarity with regard to values and allow individuals to pursue goals consistent with these values despite negative internal experiences. As such, it can be motivational and this may also be important in couples work where individuals may recognize that without some emotional discomfort in their relationship (perhaps brought on by disclosure of negative feelings), they may never reach their professed goal of an honest relationship where feelings are not hidden or expressed indirectly.

COMPASSION-FOCUSED INTERVENTIONS

Compassion has been a topic in psychotherapy research and practice for many years, but in recent years many practical therapy tools for developing compassion have emerged (Gilbert, 2010; Neff, 2011). Often the first step in helping clients develop compassion for themselves and others is to begin mindfulness practice which incorporates a loving-kindness meditation or metta meditation (from the original Sanskrit), that is aimed at developing gradually into a loving and kind concern for the well-being of oneself, valued others, enemies and all humanity.

Introduction to Metta Meditation

The client, having first practiced mindful breathing or a sitting meditation, can be instructed by the therapist in the practice of metta meditation. A handout is provided to be the basis for practice within session and as a homework assignment.

Each session does not have to include all the levels. What is most important is that it be done in a deep, leisurely way and not superficially. It is worthwhile to include oneself in every loving- kindness meditation, irrespective of who else is included, or simply to do this on its own, if time is short. It has been found that when people experience negative emotions, such as anger, they may be able to replace the anger at another person with loving kindness if they have first taken this step of showing loving kindness towards themselves. Practicing this regularly may have benefits for the relationship given that individuals can develop more understanding and compassion, to themselves and to their partner, as a result of such deliberate cultivation of feelings of loving kindness.

In conclusion, mindfulness therapies can be viewed as an extension of CBT and behavioral therapies. All use related means of bringing awareness, cognition and emotion regulation to change behavior in beneficial ways. The more you use any of these, the more you will find that you are integrating ideas from all of them. In the chapter that follows, we'll see how to integrate concepts from positive psychology into therapy.

METTA MEDITATION

Metta meditation refers to developing loving kindness towards ourselves and others. This has many benefits in terms of compassion and empathy, which have the power to positively change brain function and also benefit us in many other ways. All forms of meditation are in themselves an act of kindness to oneself and to other people, but it may be helpful to make this more explicit as you will in this practice.

Start by sitting with yourself; enjoy and focus on your breathing. As you continue to breathe in and out, and when you are ready, dwell gently with phrases such as:

> May I be happy.
>
> May I have peace and well-being.
>
> May I be free from negative emotions.
>
> May I be safe.

Take your time saying each one. Do not rush the process.

When ready and when you have begun perhaps to feel the benefits from this step, widen the circle to someone else, beginning with a person who is closest to you. Continue to breathe in and out in a relaxed, unforced way and dwell with the same phrases, this time putting in the name of the person.

> May . . . be happy.
>
> May . . . have peace and well-being.
>
> May . . . be free from negative emotions.
>
> May . . . be safe.

Then the practice can be extended in the same way to a friend, a neutral person (someone you don't know well) and eventually, with practice, to someone you have issues with or find it hard to think about without distress.

Finally, you may want to express the same intentions towards all living things.

Copyright 2018 © John W. Ludgate & Tereza N. Grubr, *The CBT Couples Toolbox*. All Rights Reserved

Some other steps in compassion development include strategies described by Neff (2011) and Germer (2009).

Neff describes compassion as involving three components:
- *Self-kindness* (which replaces self-judgment)
- *Common Humanity* (which replaces isolation)
- *Mindfulness* (which replaces over-identification)

In working with couples, the first step is to help them develop self-compassion. The steps involved in acquiring self-compassion are detailed on page 96 and this can be discussed in session. Clients will be encouraged to practice self-compassion using the form Self-Compassion Practice on page 97. Seeing the examples given of converting self-judgment to self-kindness, isolation to common humanity and over-identification to mindfulness they will each try to do this for themselves in the personal examples section by noting thoughts that occur in the categories listed, self-judgment, isolation and over-identification, and attempting to restate them in the healthier alternative, self-kindness, common humanity and mindfulness.

Having practices self-compassion regularly they are encouraged to practice compassion to each other by using the form Compassion to Others Practice on page 99 again noticing the three components, other-judgment, isolation over-identification, when they occur and turning these to the healthier alternatives, other-kindness, common humanity and mindfulness. Partners can be shown how to apply this procedure in session and then have it assigned as a homework activity.

Clients, after practicing self-compassion, will be introduced to compassion to others. The handout **Compassion to Others Practice**, (page 99) which incorporates mindfulness and acceptance of others, based on the work of Germer (2009), will now be given to both partners with instructions to practice this strategy in session and as a homework assignment.

SELF-COMPASSION SAMPLE

	Replace with	Self-kindness
Self-judgment		I am tolerant of my flaws.
When I see something in myself which I don't like, I am self-critical.		
	Replace with	**Common Humanity**
Isolation		When I feel inadequate I remind myself that many people feel this way sometimes.
When I feel down I think most people are happier than me.		
	Replace with	**Mindfulness**
Over-identification		When I am upset I try to approach my feelings with openness and curiosity.
When I feel down I obsess and fixate on how I feel.		

Copyright 2018 © John W. Ludgate & Tereza N. Grubr, *The CBT Couples Toolbox*. All Rights Reserved

SELF-COMPASSION PRACTICE

	Self-kindness	Replace with	Self-judgment
	Common Humanity	Replace with	Isolation
	Mindfulness	Replace with	Over-identification

Copyright 2018 © John W. Ludgate & Tereza N. Grubr, *The CBT Couples Toolbox*. All Rights Reserved

COMPASSION TO OTHER SAMPLE

Other judgment		**Replace with**	**Other kindness**
When I see something in my partner which I don't like, I am critical.			I am tolerant of his/her flaws.
Isolation		**Replace with**	**Common Humanity**
When our relationship is not so good I think most people are happier than us.			When I feel this I remind myself that many couples probably feel this way sometimes.
Over-identification		**Replace with**	**Mindfulness**
When I feel down about us, I obsess and fixate on how I feel and what needs to be done.			When I am upset about what is going on with us, I try to approach my feelings with openness and curiosity.

Copyright 2018 © John W. Ludgate & Tereza N. Grubr, *The CBT Couples Toolbox*. All Rights Reserved

COMPASSION TO OTHER PRACTICE

Other judgment		Other kindness	Replace with			
Isolation		Common Humanity	Replace with			
Over-identification		Mindfulness	Replace with			

Copyright 2018 © John W. Ludgate & Tereza N. Grubr, *The CBT Couples Toolbox*. All Rights Reserved

STEPS TO
SELF-COMPASSION

Soften into your body:

- Care for yourself physically
- Relax, don't tense
- Soothe the body

Allow your thoughts:

- Care for yourself mentally
- Cut out judgment and self-criticism, allow thoughts to come and go
- Visualize your thoughts moving like a stream or waves on an ocean
- Develop compassion for your own thoughts and for your brain

Befriend your feelings:

- Stop fighting feelings
- Accept what is
- Show empathy and compassion to the person having the feelings
- Practice loving-kindness or metta meditation
- Engage in self-forgiveness, as necessary
- Engage in relaxing or pleasurable activities

Relate to others:

- Connect with others to prevent isolation
- Show kindness, compassion and gratitude to others

Nourish your spirit:

- Cultivate closeness to a transcendent being
- Create intimate contact with the miracle of everyday life
- Develop appreciation of everyday miracles with a corresponding decrease in "selfing" or self-enlargement

Copyright 2018 © John W. Ludgate & Tereza N. Grubr, *The CBT Couples Toolbox*. All Rights Reserved

CHAPTER 6:
Positive Psychology Interventions

Positive Psychology, which was developed by psychologist Martin Seligman, is "the scientific and applied approach to uncovering people's strengths and promoting their positive functioning" (Lopez, Pedrotti, & Snyder, 2015). While classical areas of psychology and psychiatry in the 20th century focused predominantly on understanding and treating mental illness, Positive Psychology as a field has sought to study not only people's weaknesses, but also their strengths. In recent years, Positive Psychology has shown to be an approach able to help individuals enhance their well-being and decrease their unhappiness, by providing evidence-based approaches and resources that practitioners can use with their clients.

Research in the field of Positive Psychology (Sin & Lyubomirsky, 2009) shows that:

- Individuals expecting Positive Psychology interventions to make them happier tend to benefit most from them, especially when they are motivated and encouraged by their therapist/psychologist.

- Positive psychological interventions have proven to be most useful in long-term therapy with longer-lasting interventions. The result is in greater increases in individual well-being, as clients are able to turn the activities they have learned into daily habits.

- Engaging in multiple Positive Psychology interventions has shown to be more effective than engaging in only one activity.

Although positive psychology interventions have been describes and evaluated largely in the field of individual therapy, it would seem obvious that strategies which focus on cultivating positive cognitions, feelings and behaviors and which come from a model which emphasizes strengthens rather than problems can be utilized successfully with relationship problems. As stated previously distressed relationships often involve negative cognitions and negative behavioral exchanges so a reversal of this tendency is likely to be helpful in renegotiating healthy relationships.

Most of the exercises and practices in this chapter were inspired by the work of Ben-Shahar (2010), a significant figure in positive psychology, and author of the book *Even Happier*, which is a guided journal based on positive psychology research and aimed at helping people increase their happiness, or subjective well-being.

Positive Psychology Interventions include following seven key categories below. Each of these are explored more deeply and addressed with helpful tools and practices through the chapter:

- Gratitude exercises
- Strengths assessment
- Forgiveness exercises
- Creating meaningfulness
- Self-care and rituals
- Benevolence exercises
- Resiliency and emotion-focused coping

GRATITUDE EXERCISES

The concept of gratitude is an important aspect of positive psychology. Emmons & McCullough (2004) state that gratitude surfaces when an individual recognizes that they have acquired a positive outcome from another person, that is the other person behaved in a way that was costly to them, somehow valuable to the recipient of the action, and intentionally given.

Research shows that:

- Gratitude is connected to the tendency and ability to enjoy and appreciate everyday experiences and events (Lopez, Pedrotti, & Snyder, 2015).
- Gratitude can enhance relationship quality and significance in dynamic ways.
- The assessment of the self-other relationship is strongly correlated with action tendencies that focus on the building of relationships, oftentimes with the presence of significant affect and a strong experience of oneness and identity.
- Shifts in self-other boundaries in connection to gratitude are linked to positive emotions, creative responses to the perceived benefits of feeling grateful, and consistent enhancement patterns in both self and other relationships.
- The depth and frequency of gratitude experienced by individuals within their relationships is associated with deep states of immersion, awe and relationship satisfaction.
- Participants in such studies describe the feeling of gratitude as a combination of somatic sensations and a variety of emotions, including love, joy, awe, warmth, release and blessedness (Hlava & Elfers, 2014).

Additionally, research studies on the effect of gratitude on people's psychological and physical well-being (Emmons & McCullough, 2003) show the following:

- Weekly gratitude listings result in more optimistic and positive evaluations of life, more exercise, and fewer physical symptoms.
- Daily self-guided gratitude exercises lead to higher reported levels of positive affect, as well as an increased likelihood of helping others or offering emotional support, which suggests that one of the results of gratitude exercises can be an increase in prosocial and moral motivation.
- Individuals engaged in practicing gratitude showed higher levels of positive affect, more and better sleep, an increase in optimism, and a feeling of connectedness with others.

There are numerous reasons for practicing gratitude with clients in couples therapy, as can be clearly seen in the above mentioned research findings. Ben-Shahar (2010) suggests that practicing gratitude can lead to the following benefits:

- When individuals make it a habit to realize what they are grateful for, they do not need special events to make them happy; instead, they become increasingly aware of the good things that happen to them on a daily basis.
- Expressing gratitude in a relationship can lead to an increase in awareness of the positive aspects of the relationship, as well as an increase in mutual appreciation of one's partner and life in general.
- Gratitude also tends to lead to an increase in well-being, happiness, determination, optimism, energy, fewer symptoms of physical illness, better sleep, and a propensity to exercise more.
- Practicing gratitude tends to contribute to individuals becoming more generous and supportive of others; such benefits are likely to be seen when gratitude is used in couples therapy.

You can introduce the following worksheet, Warm-Up Gratitude Exercise, to couples after the topic of gratitude and the benefits of practicing are outlined. It can be used to facilitate gratitude either in session or as a homework assignment. After the **Warm-Up Gratitude Exercise**, another worksheet is provided called **Daily Partnership Gratitude List**.

WARM-UP GRATITUDE EXERCISE

What are you grateful for in your partner? What are some of the things you appreciate about him/her?

_____

_____

_____

_____

_____

_____

_____

_____

_____

_____

_____

_____

_____

_____

Copyright 2018 © John W. Ludgate & Tereza N. Grubr, *The CBT Couples Toolbox*. All Rights Reserved

DAILY PARTNERSHIP GRATITUDE LIST

- For every day of this week, make a list of at least five qualities you are grateful for in your partner.

- As this gratitude exercise becomes a habit, your awareness of what you're grateful for will increase.

- If you have trouble coming up with things you appreciate about your partner, remember to be mindful, which you can do by trying to visualize and/or experience what you are grateful for.

- After this initial week, it is helpful to continue reminding yourself what you are grateful for in your partner once a week.

- You may even start a gratitude journal for your relationship, where you can document your gratitude exercises.

Monday: In my partner, I am grateful for. . .

_____

_____

Tuesday: In my partner, I am grateful for. . .

_____

_____

Wednesday: In my partner, I am grateful for. . .

_____

_____

Thursday: In my partner, I am grateful for. . .

_____

_____

Copyright 2018 © John W. Ludgate & Tereza N. Grubr, *The CBT Couples Toolbox*. All Rights Reserved

Friday: In my partner, I am grateful for. . .

_____

_____

Saturday: In my partner, I am grateful for. . .

_____

_____

Sunday: In my partner, I am grateful for. . .

_____

_____

WEEKLY PARTNERSHIP GRATITUDE LIST:

This week, I am grateful for this in my partner:

_____

_____

_____

_____

_____

Copyright 2018 © John W. Ludgate & Tereza N. Grubr, *The CBT Couples Toolbox*. All Rights Reserved

STRENGTHS ASSESSMENT

Positive psychology stresses the importance of clients recognizing strengths, skills and resilience. Research (Lopez, Pedrotti, & Synder, 2015) demonstrates that:

- Some of the **most effective individuals** are the ones who **understand their own strengths,** a finding reported by the Gallup Organization.

- People who possess an understanding of their strengths are most capable of developing different strategies to not only meet the demands of daily life, careers and personal relationships, but also to exceed them.

- Understanding and awareness of one's strengths can provide insight into why one is successful.

- **Learning about personal strengths** tends to result in a **boost of confidence and positive emotions about oneself**; strength work has also been associated with an **increase in subjective well-being.**

Some added benefits of a strengths assessment are that individuals can identify their talents and subsequently build them into strengths, as well as enjoy the success that arises from utilizing their strengths.

In the area of couples therapy, identifying one's partner's strengths as well as one's own can be extremely beneficial to the relationship and to personal well-being.

The following **Strengths Assessment Exercise** helps each partner realize their own strengths, identify their partner's strengths, and determine which strengths make their relationship work.

STRENGTHS ASSESSMENT EXERCISE

What are your five main strengths?

1. _____

2. _____

3. _____

4. _____

5. _____

What are your partner's five main strengths?

1. _____

2. _____

3. _____

4. _____

5. _____

Which five main strengths do you think your partner would say you possess?

1. _____

2. _____

3. _____

4. _____

5. _____

What are your five main strengths as a couple?

1. _____

2. _____

3. _____

4. _____

5. _____

Copyright 2018 © John W. Ludgate & Tereza N. Grubr, *The CBT Couples Toolbox*. All Rights Reserved

How can you work on improving both your individual strengths and the strengths you possess as a couple?

Improvement of Individual Strengths

_____

_____

_____

_____

_____

Improvement of Mutual Relationship Strengths

_____

_____

_____

_____

_____

Copyright 2018 © John W. Ludgate & Tereza N. Grubr, *The CBT Couples Toolbox*. All Rights Reserved

FORGIVENESS EXERCISES

Enright, Freedman, and Rique (1998) defined forgiveness as "a willingness to abandon one's right to resentment, negative judgment, and indifferent behavior toward one who unjustly hurt us, while fostering the undeserved qualities of compassion, generosity, and even love toward him or her."

Specifically, forgiveness can result in:

- Being freed from holding a grudge (Thompson et al., 2005).
- Increases in prosocial motivation towards others in that there is less desire to avoid the person who has transgressed, and an increased desire to display positive behavior towards a transgressor, with signs of *increased benevolence over time* (McCullough et al., 2000).

Steps in forgiving another person

The forgiveness model developed by Gordon, Baucom, and Snyder (2005) has been found useful in working with couples struggling with forgiveness issues. In this model, **forgiveness is the GOAL**, and there are several steps in achieving it.

- Promoting a realistic appraisal of the relationship between the couple.
- Attempting to facilitate a release from ruminating and negative affect toward the partner who has violated/transgressed.
- Helping the victimized partner in lessening his/her desire to punish the transgressor.

It has been found that, gradually, forgiveness helps the negative feelings and hurt decrease/diminish, especially for the wronged partner. This approach **enhances empathy** for the transgressing partner/the "culprit," while you attempt to help both partners feel better about themselves.

Forgiveness stages are similar to trauma recovery stages in that the couple moves gradually from the impact stage, to the search for meaning or understanding of the incident stage, and eventually to the recovery stage, in which they resume normal functioning.

- The **initial impact stage** usually entails many negative emotions and quick changes in feelings/moods.
- The **meaning stage** is characterized by trying to understand why the event (e.g. an affair) happened.
- The **final stage** is where the partners usually regain control over their lives.

It is crucial that you continually remind the couple that the event cannot be in control of their daily life. Also, the couple needs to understand that forgiveness does not necessarily mean staying together (that is a separate decision to be made), but does involve a greater awareness and knowledge that will help them to move forward, whichever decision they make.

Another model of forgiveness with couples therapy implications is that of Everett Worthington (1998). This involves helping the couple through five steps based on the acronym **REACH.**

These are:

- Encourage the partners to **Recall** the hurt and nature of the injury caused.
- Promote **Empathy** in both partners and help them reach it.
- **Altruistically** help the partners give each other the gift of forgiveness.
- Help the partners to **Commit** verbally to forgive.
- Help the partners to **Hold** onto that forgiveness for each other.

Encourage the couple to practice the following **Forgiveness Exercise**.

FORGIVENESS EXERCISE

Think of a time recently when you became upset with your partner based on some action or behavior of his/hers.

What occurred (what was said or done)?

_____

_____

What impact did it have on your feelings?

_____

_____

Why might this have occurred (what was going on for your partner)?

_____

_____

Can you accept or forgive your partner for this?

_____

_____

What can you say verbally to indicate forgiveness or acceptance?

_____

_____

What response might you get from your partner if you do this?

_____

_____

What will be the overall consequence for your relationship if you forgive your partner?

_____

_____

Copyright 2018 © John W. Ludgate & Tereza N. Grubr, *The CBT Couples Toolbox*. All Rights Reserved

MEANINGFULNESS IN DAILY LIFE AND IN PARTNERSHIP

Another aspect of positive psychology that can have an impact in couples counseling is helping clients find meaning in their lives and in their relationship.

You can introduce this concept and its importance, and then proceed to introduce the following homework exercise:

Steps:

- Instruct each partner separately to record their daily activities for a week using the worksheet on the next page, including approximate time periods spent on those activities, to acquire a sense of what each of the partner's week comprises (Ben-Shahar, 2010).

  - Make sure the partners differentiate between the activities they do together and those they do separately.

- After one week, during your next session, have both partners fill out the table on page 111 with the activities that took place on each day of week, how much pleasure and meaning these activities resulted in, and the amount of time they spent doing them.

- Have the partners rate their satisfaction with both their individual and couple activities.
  Then, instruct the partners to establish whether they would like to spend more or less time on each particular activity.

  - If the partners would like to spend more time on the activity, have them put a "+" next to it, or "++" if they would like to spend even more time doing it.

  - If the partners would like to spend less time partaking in a certain activity, have them put a "-"; if they would like to spend even less time on an activity, have them put "- -" next to it.

  - If the partners are satisfied with the amount of time they spend on a specific activity, have them write "=" next to that activity.

  - Let the partners rate the satisfaction derived from that particular activity, on a scale from 1 to 5.

- Let the partners discuss if an increase in certain activities would make them happier, both as individuals and as a couple.

  - Help the partners explore those activities that do not yield as much happiness, both individually and collectively, and see if they could be diminished or stopped altogether.

Individual Chart for Recording Meaningful Activities

	Individual weekly activities and evaluation of their meaning and satisfaction			
	Activity done individually (working, cleaning, exercising, reading, etc.)	Amount of time spent on activity (approximate)	Desire to spend more/less/same amount of time on this activity (=, +, ++, -, or - -)	Satisfaction derived from this activity (scale from 1 to 5)	Ideas on how to increase satisfactory activities/decrease undesirable activities
Monday					
Tuesday					
Wednesday					
Thursday					
Friday					
Saturday					
Sunday					

Copyright 2018 © John W. Ludgate & Tereza N. Grubr, *The CBT Couples Toolbox*. All Rights Reserved

COUPLES CHART FOR RECORDING MEANINGFUL ACTIVITIES

Weekly couple activities and evaluation of their meaning and satisfaction

	Activity done as a couple (going out, eating together, sexual activities, etc.)	Amount of time spent on activity (approximate)	Desire to spend more/less/same amount of time on this activity (=, +, ++, -, or - -)	Satisfaction derived from this activity (scale from 1 to 5)	Ideas on how to increase satisfactory activities/decrease undesirable activities
Monday					
Tuesday					
Wednesday					
Thursday					
Friday					
Saturday					
Sunday					

Copyright 2018 © John W. Ludgate & Tereza N. Grubr, *The CBT Couples Toolbox*. All Rights Reserved

Together, as a couple, make a list of weekly activities that you could newly engage in and that would make your relationship more satisfactory.

_____

_____

_____

_____

_____

_____

_____

_____

_____

_____

_____

_____

_____

_____

_____

_____

_____

_____

_____

_____

Copyright 2018 © John W. Ludgate & Tereza N. Grubr, *The CBT Couples Toolbox*. All Rights Reserved

SELF-CARE INVOLVING POSITIVE HABITS AND RITUALS

To effectively include this important intervention in couples work, you will want to understand and cover the following:

- Concept of rituals and positive habits to clients. These play an important role, not just in self-care, but in promoting mutual care in the relationship (Ben-Shahar, 2010).

  Examples of rituals could include:
  - morning coffee together
  - going over the events of the day together
  - planning weekend events together
- Emphasize the importance of initiating and maintaining both individual and couple rituals to clients.
- Help the couple define the exact behaviors their rituals consist of, and how these behaviors impact their relationship.
- Explore with the couple the values connected to these rituals and the background connected to the importance of these rituals (for example, observation of family rituals that the client perceived to have benefits for them or others).

Ask your clients to complete the following **Exercise in Developing Positive Habits and Rituals** together as a homework assignment.

EXERCISE IN DEVELOPING
POSITIVE HABITS AND RITUALS

Develop two new rituals as a couple that you think would make your relationship a better one. What are they and how can you implement them in your relationship?

New ritual 1:

_____

_____

_____

_____

New ritual 2:

_____

_____

_____

_____

Carry out these rituals for a month and then explore how they have changed your relationship. Do you see improvement? If so, in which areas of your relationship?

_____

_____

_____

_____

_____

Copyright 2018 © John W. Ludgate & Tereza N. Grubr, *The CBT Couples Toolbox*. All Rights Reserved

BENEVOLENCE

Benevolence has been defined as the disposition to do good for others, or as an act of kindness or a generous gift. Studies in the field of positive psychology have shown that benevolence and giving to others can increase our overall well-being. Based on these findings, we recommend incorporating benevolence exercises into couples' work. Incorporating the practice of benevolence in couples' therapy is beneficial because it increases interpersonal satisfaction and relationship quality.

You can discuss this concept with the couple and use the following **Benevolence Exercise** worksheet, which is based on an approach by Ben-Shahar (2010).

BENEVOLENCE EXERCISE

Try to recall a time when you were helpful towards your partner and felt appreciated for that gesture. Think about how your partner responded to it and how you felt as a result of that. Try to experience those emotions again. Ponder your general outlook on giving to your partner and also receiving from him/her. How does that make you feel?

Act of benevolence/generosity towards your partner:

Situation:

_____

_____

Partner's response:

_____

_____

Your emotions:

_____

_____

Impact on relationship:

_____

_____

Try to imagine a future situation with your partner in which you are helpful, benevolent, and caring. Think of the emotional response attached to this act and try to experience it in your mind and body.

Take time to think about acts of benevolence and generosity on a regular basis, and to re-experience the emotions elicited by those acts.

What other helpful and generous acts towards your partner could you partake in?

Possible future acts of benevolence/generosity:

_____

_____

_____

Copyright 2018 © John W. Ludgate & Tereza N. Grubr, *The CBT Couples Toolbox*. All Rights Reserved

NEGATIVE EMOTIONS, RESILIENCE AND EMOTION-FOCUSED COPING

Research (Stanton et al., 2009) has shown the usefulness of emotion-focused coping, which is actively moving toward a stressful encounter and employing "appetitive motivation." Appetitive motivation promotes behaviors that encourage approach, as opposed to avoidance, and are aimed at achieving a reward or positive outcome. This can help individuals realize the emotional and behavioral rewards arising from a given situation.

It has been found (Lopez, Pedrotti, & Snyder, 2015) that positively reframing a situation that is part of emotion-focused coping can help individuals to:

- Retain positive feelings about themselves, increase well-being, and decrease stress levels.
- Better understand what they are experiencing and redirect attention to central concerns in their lives.
- Face future stressors directly, instead of avoiding them.
- Deal with stressors repeatedly, which leads to habituation developing to predictable negative life experiences.

Research findings (Fredrickson, Tugade, Waugh, & Larkin, 2003) also show that:

- Positive emotions often occur along with negative ones during stressful situations.
- Individuals who experience positive emotions in difficult times are more likely to find positive meaning in their negative experience, along with developing long-term goals and plans following the stressful event.
- The experience of positive emotions leads to the permanent acquisition of personal resources; additionally, experiencing positive emotions can help individuals become healthier, more resilient, knowledgeable, and socially integrated, as well as better prepared to cope with future difficulties.
- Experiencing positive emotions builds survival resources by broadening awareness and creating a temporary form of consciousness that entails a wider range of thoughts, perceptions and actions than one would experience under normal circumstances.

When working with a couple on positive reframing, you can:

- Encourage both individuals to think of a situation that they view as negative or difficult in their relationship.
- Have both of them explore the same situation using the worksheet on the next page and then do the same with other examples of negative experiences.
- The couple should be encouraged to begin thinking more positively about negative events in their relationship. This will also help them handle future difficulties more easily and with more positive, rather than negative, thoughts occurring.

The worksheet **Transforming Negative Experiences in the Relationship into More Positive Ones** can prompt the clients to use this approach to practice, both in session and between sessions, positively reframing negative experiences when they occur in the relationship.

TRANSFORMING NEGATIVE EXPERIENCES IN THE RELATIONSHIP INTO MORE POSITIVE ONES

Describe a negative/stressful experience in the relationship:

_____

_____

_____

What are the negative emotions arising from this situation?

_____

_____

_____

What are the positive emotions arising from this situation?

_____

_____

_____

Develop meaning derived from this experience:

_____

_____

_____

Describe how a similar situation could be approached in the future in a more positive way:

_____

_____

_____

Copyright 2018 © John W. Ludgate & Tereza N. Grubr, *The CBT Couples Toolbox*. All Rights Reserved

Resources for Special Issues in Working with Couples

PARTNER VIOLENCE

Murphy, C.M. & Eckhardt, C.I. (2005). *Treating the Abusive Partner: An Individualized Cognitive Behavioral Approach.* New York: Guilford Press.

Stith, S.M., McCullum, E.E., & Rosen, K.H. (2011). *Couples Therapy for Domestic Violence: Finding Safe Solutions.* Washington, DC: American Psychological Association.

INFIDELITY

Snyder, D., Baucom, D., & Gordon, K. (2007). *Getting Past the Affair.* New York: Guilford Press.

Spring, J.A. (2005). *How Can I Forgive You?* New York: William Morrow Paperback.

SEXUAL DYSFUNCTION

McCarthy, B. & McCarthy, E. (1998). *Couple Sexual Awareness: Building Sexual Happiness.* New York: Carrol & Graf.

Leiblum, S.R. (2006). *Principles and Practice of Sex Therapy (4th ed.).* New York: Guilford Press.

DIVORCE

Fisher, B. & Alberti, R. (1999). *Rebuilding: When Your Relationship Ends (3rd ed.).* New York: Impact Press.

Lebow, J.L. (2015). Separation and divorce issues in couple therapy. In A.S. Gurman & J.L. Lebow (Eds.), *Clinical Handbook of Couple Therapy.* New York: Guilford Press.

MARITAL DISCORD AND CO-OCCURRING DISORDERS

Lebow, J.L. (2015). Separation and divorce issues in couple therapy. In A.S. Gurman & J.L. Lebow (Eds.), *Clinical handbook of couple therapy.* New York: Guilford Press.

WORKING WITH LGBT COUPLES

Green, R.J. & Mitchell, V. (2015). *Gay, Lesbian, and Bisexual Issues in Couple Therapy.* In A.S. Gurman & J.L. Lebow (Eds.), *Clinical Handbook of Couple Therapy.* New York: Guilford Press.

Recommended Readings

ASSESSMENT OF COUPLES (CHAPTER 1)

Dattilio, F. (2010). *Cognitive Behavioral Therapy with Couples and Families: A Comprehensive Guide for Clinicians.* Chapter 5. New York: Guilford Press.

Fischer, J. & Corcoran, K. (1994). *Measures for Clinical Practice. Volume 1. Instruments for Couples, Families and Children.* New York: Free Press.

MOTIVATIONAL INTERVIEWING (CHAPTER 2)

Miller, W. R. & Rollnick, S. (2013). *Motivational Interviewing (3rd Ed.).* New York: Guilford Press.

Zuckoff, A. (2015). *Finding Your Way To Change.* New York: Guilford Press.

CBT (CHAPTER 3)

Beck, A. T. (1988). *Love is Never Enough.* New York: Harper & Row.

Dattilio, F. (2010). *Cognitive Behavioral Therapy with Couples and Families: A Comprehensive Guide for Clinicians.* New York: Guilford Press.

Dattilio, F. & Padesky, C. (1990). *Cognitive Therapy with Couples.* Sarasota, FL: Professional Resources Exchange.

BEHAVIORAL TECHNIQUES (CHAPTER 4)

Christensen, A. & Jacobson, N. (2001). *Reconcilable Differences.* New York: Guilford Press.

Epstein, N. & Baucom, D. (2002). *Enhanced Cognitive Behavioral Therapy for Couples: A Contextual Approach.* Washington, DC: American Psychological Association.

DBT (CHAPTER 5)

Fruzetti, A. (2006). *The High Conflict Couple: A Dialectical Behavior Therapy Guide to Finding Peace, Intimacy and Validation.* Oakland, CA: New Harbinger Publications, Inc.

Linehan, M.M. (1993). *Cognitive Behavioral Treatment of Borderline Personality Disorder.* New York: Guilford Press.

MINDFULNESS (CHAPTER 5)

Germer, C. (2009). *The Mindful Path to Self-Compassion: Freeing Yourself from Destructive Thoughts and Emotions.* New York: Guilford Press.

Kabat-Zinn, J. (1990). *Full Catastrophe Living.* New York: Bantam.

ACCEPTANCE AND COMMITMENT THERAPY (CHAPTER 5)

Gehart, D.R. (2012). *Mindfulness and Acceptance in Couple and Family Therapy.* New York: Springer.

Walser, R.D. & Westrup, D. (2009). *The Mindful Couple: How Acceptance and Mindfulness Can Lead You to the Love You Want.* Oakland, CA: New Harbinger Publications, Inc.

COMPASSION-FOCUSED THERAPY (CHAPTER 5)

Gilbert, P. (2010). *The Compassionate Mind: A New Approach to Life's Challenges.* Oakland, CA: New Harbinger Publications, Inc.

Neff, K. (2015). *Self-Compassion: The Proven Power of Being Kind to Yourself.* New York: William Morrow.

POSITIVE PSYCHOLOGY (CHAPTER 6)

Ben-Shahar, T. (2010). *Even Happier: A Gratitude Journal for Daily Joy and Lasting Fulfillment.* New York: McGraw-Hill.

Lopez, S. J., Pedrotti, J. T. & Snyder, C. R. (2015). *Positive Psychology: The Scientific and Practical Explorations of Human Strengths (3rd ed.).* Thousand Oaks, CA: Sage Publications, Inc.

References

For your convenience, purchasers can download and print worksheets and handouts from www.pesi.com/CBTCouples

Arkowitz, H., Miller, W. R. & Rollnick, S. (Eds.). (2015). *Motivational Interviewing in the Treatment of Psychological Problems. Second Edition*. New York: Guilford Press.

Azrin, N.H., Naster, B.J. & Jones, R. (1973). Reciprocity counseling: A rapid learning-based procedure for marital counseling. *Behavior Research and Therapy*, 11, 365-382.

Barnes, S., Brown, K.W., Krusemark, E., Campbell, W.K. & Rugge, R.D. (2007). The role of mindfulness in romantic relationship satisfaction and response to relationship stress. *Journal of Marital & Family Therapy*, 33,(4), 482-500.

Beck, A. T. (1988). *Love is Never Enough*. New York: Harper & Row.

Bedrosian, R. & Bozicas, G. (1994). *Treating Family of Origin Problems: A Cognitive Approach*. New York: Guilford.

"Benevolence." (2016). *Merriam-Webster.com*. Merriam-Webster, n.d. http://www.merriam-webster.com/dictionary/benevolence

Ben-Shahar, T. (2010). *Even Happier: A Gratitude Journal for Daily Joy and Lasting Fulfillment*. New York: McGraw-Hill.

Burns, D. D. (2008). *Feeling Good Together: The Secret to Making Troubled Relationships Work*. New York: Broadway Books.

Carson, J., Carson, K.M., Gill, K.M. & Baucom, D.H. (2004). Mindfulness-based relationship enhancement. *Behavior Therapy*, 35, 471-494.

Christensen, A. (1988). Dysfunctional interaction patterns in couples. In P. Noller & M.A. Fitzpatrick (Eds.), *Perspectives on Marital Interactions*. Clevendon, UK: Multilingual Matters.

Christensen, A. & Jacobson, N. (2001). *Reconcilable Differences*. New York: Guilford Press.

Dattilio, F. (2010). *Cognitive Behavioral Therapy with Couples and Families: A Comprehensive Guide for Clinicians*. New York: Guilford Press.

Dattilio, F. & Padesky, C. (1990). *Cognitive Therapy with Couples*. Professional Resources Exchange.

Eidelson, F.I. & Epstein, N. (1982). Cognition and relationship maladjustment: Development of a measure of dysfunctional relationship beliefs. *Journal of Consulting and Clinical Psychology*, 50, 715-720.

Emmons, R.A. & McCullough, M.E. (Eds.). (2004). *The Psychology of Gratitude*. New York: Oxford University Press.

Emmons, R.A. & McCullough, M.E. (2003). Counting blessings versus burdens: An experimental investigation of gratitude and subjective well-being in daily life. *Journal of Personality and Social Psychology*, 84(2), 377–389.

Enright, R.D., Freedman, S. & Rique, J. (1998). The psychology of interpersonal forgiveness. In R.D. Enright & J. North (Eds.), *Exploring Forgiveness* (pp.46-62). Madison, WI: University of Wisconsin Press.

Epstein, N. & Baucom, D. (2002). *Enhanced Cognitive Behavioral Therapy for Couples: A Contextual Approach*. Washington, DC: American Psychological Association.

Epstein, N. et al (Ed.). (1988). *Cognitive Behavioral Therapy with Families*. New York: Bruner-Mazel.

Fischer, J. & Corcoran, K. (1994). *Measures for Clinical Practice. Volume 1. Instruments for Couples, Families and Children*. New York: Free Press.

Fredrickson, B. L. (2013). Updated thinking on positivity ratios. *American Psychologist*, 68, 1–10.

Fredrickson, B. L., Tugade, M. M., Waugh, C. E. & Larkin, G. R. (2003). What good are positive emotions in crises?: A prospective study of resilience and emotions following the terrorist attacks on the United States on September 11, 2001. *Journal of Personality and Social Psychology*, 84 (2), 365–376.

Gehart, D.R. (2012). *Mindfulness and Acceptance in Couple and Family Therapy*. New York: Springer.

Germer, C. (2009). *The Mindful Path to Self-Compassion: Freeing Yourself from Destructive Thoughts and Emotions*. New York: Guilford.

Gilbert, P. (2010). *The Compassionate Mind; A New Approach to Life's Challenges*. Oakland, CA: New Harbinger.

Gordon, K.C., Baucom, D.H. & Snyder, D.K. (2005). Forgiveness in couples: Divorce, infidelity, and couples therapy. In E. Worthington (Ed.), *Handbook of Forgiveness* (pp. 407-422). New York: Routledge.

Gottman, J. M. (1994). *What Predicts Divorce*. Hillsdale, NJ: Erlbaum.

Gottman, J. M. & Gottman, J. S. (1999). Marital survival kit: A research-based marital therapy. In R. Berger & M.T. Hannah (Eds.), *Preventive Approaches in Couples Therapy*. New York: Bruner–Mazel.

Hayes, S., Strosahl, K. & Wilson, K. (1994). *Acceptance and Commitment Therapy: The Process and Practice of Mindful Change*. New York: Guilford Press.

Hlava, P. & Elfers, J. (2014). The lived experience of gratitude. *Journal of Humanistic Psychology*, 54 (4), 434-455.

Jacobsen, N. S. & Margolin, G. (1979). *Marital Therapy: Strategies Based on Social Learning and Behavior Exchange Principles*. New York: Bruner-Mazel.

Kabat-Zinn, J. (1990). *Full Catastrophe Living*. New York: Bantam.

Lopez, S. J., Pedrotti, J. T. & Snyder, C. R. (2015). *Positive Psychology: The Scientific and Practical Explorations of Human Strengths (3rd Ed.)*. Thousand Oaks, CA: Sage.

Marra, T. (2004). *Depressed & Anxious: The Dialectical Behavior Therapy Workbook for Overcoming Depression and Anxiety*. Oakland, CA: New Harbinger.

Mates-Youngman, K. (2014). *Couples Therapy Workbook: 30 Guided Converstaions to Re-connect Relationships*. Eau Claire, WI: PESI Publishing & Media.

McCullough, M.E., Pargament, K.I. & Thoresen, C.E. (Eds.). (2000a). *Forgiveness: Theory, Research, and Practice*. New York: Guilford Press.

Miller, W. R. & Rollnick, S. (2013). *Motivational Interviewing: Helping People Change*. New York: Guilford Press.

Neff, K. (2015). *Self-Compassion: The Proven Power of Being Kind to Yourself*. New York: William Morrow.

Nezu, A., Nezu, C. & D'Zurilla, T. (2013). *Problem-Solving Therapy: Treatment Manual*. New York: Springer.

Persons, J. B. (1989). *Cognitive Therapy in Practice: A Case Formaulation Approach*. New York: W.W. Norton.

Prochaska, J. O. & DiClemente, C. C. (1984). *The Transtheoretical Approach: Crossing Traditional Boundaries of Therapy*. Homewood, IL: Dow Jones/Irwin.

Rathus, J. & Miller, A. (2014). *DBT Skills Manual for Adolescents*. New York: Guilford Press.

Seligman, M. P. & Csikszentmihalyi, M. (2000). Positive psychology: An introduction. *American Psychologist*, 55(1), 5-14.

Sin, N. L. & Lyubomirsky, S. (2009). Enhancing well-being and alleviating depressive symptoms with positive psychology interventions: A practice-friendly meta-analysis. *Journal of Clinical Psychology*, 65(5), 467–487.

Snyder, D.K. & Aikman, G.G. (1999). The Marital Satisfaction Inventory-Revised. In M.E. Maurish (Ed.), *Use of Psychological Testing for Treatment Planning and Outcomes Assessment*. Mahwah, NJ: Erlbaum.

Spanier, G.B. (1976). Measuring dyadic adjustment: New scales for assessing the quality of marriage and similar dyads. *Journal of Marriage and the Family*, 38, 15-28.

Stanton, A.L., Sullivan, S.J. & Austenfeld, J.L. (2009). Coping through emotional approach: Emerging evidence for the utility of processing and expressing emotions in responding to stressors. In S.J. Lopez & C.R. Snyder (Eds.), *Oxford Handbook of Positive Psychology* (pp. 225-235). New York: Oxford University Press.

Stuart, R. B. (1969). Operant-interpersonal treatment for marital discord. *Journal of Consulting & Clinical Psychology*, 33, 675-682.

Stuart, R. B. (1980). *Helping Couples Change: A Social Learning Approach to Marital Therapy*. New York: Guilford Press.

Thompson, L.Y., Snyder, C.R., Hoffman, L., Michael, S.T., Rasmussen, H.N., Billings, L.S. & Roberts, D.E. (2005). Dispositional forgiveness of self, others, and situations: The heartland forgivness scale. *Journal of Personality*, 73, 313-359.

Walser, R.D. & Westrup, D. (2009). *The Mindful Couple: How Acceptance and Mindfulness Can Lead You to the Love You Want*. Oakland, CA: New Harbinger.

Worthington, E. L. (1998). *Dimensions of Forgiveness: Psychological Research and Theological Perspectives*. West Conshohocken, PA: Templeton Foundation Press.

Zuckoff, A. (2015). *Finding Your Way to Change*. New York: Guilford Press.

Made in the USA
Las Vegas, NV
02 October 2021

31563036R00077